Exploring Grammar in Writing

upper-intermediate and advanced

with answers

Rebecca Hughes

CAMBRIDGE UNIVERSITY PRESS
Cambridge, New York, Melbourne, Madrid, Cape Town, Singapore, São Paulo

Cambridge University Press
The Edinburgh Building, Cambridge CB2 2RU, UK

www.cambridge.org
Information on this title: www.cambridge.org/9780521669948

First published 2005
Reprinted 2006

Printed in Dubai by Oriental Press

A catalogue record for this publication is available from the British Library

ISBN-13 978-0-521-66994-8
ISBN-10 0-521-66994-4

Contents

Part 3 Adding more information to the sentence

Part 4 Sequencing and focusing

Acknowledgements

I owe a debt of gratitude to many members of the Cambridge University Press ELT Divison for their patience, good humour and professionalism in what became an extended writing process for this title. I would like to thank Alison Sharpe in particular for her original faith in the project and continued support. Her sensitive, insightful and sometimes necessarily stern approach helped me considerably through some of the early iterations of the book. Jamie Smith provided an excellent new pair of eyes on the close to final versions, always providing nice (in the older sense of the word) judgements between the abstract and the practical. I owe Fiona Davis a particular debt of gratitude for her meticulous and sympathetic approach to the editing. Despite time pressures the editorial team at the Press, and Fiona most of all, have always found time to tease out a solution to a knotty problem that manages to remain in harmony with my intentions for the book. Thanks to Olly, too, for sleeping when he should (on the whole!) and providing us with a cheering topic of conversation when it all got a bit much.

Comments from students, and conversations with staff, at the Centre for English Language Education (CELE), University of Nottingham about trying to explain grammar in context have, as ever, been invaluable. I hope they will find this user-friendly, and worth the wait.

The unusually high number of ephemeral and everyday texts used in this book has meant that the process of clearing permissions has been complex and demanding. Again, particular thanks to Jamie, Fiona, Marie Allan and Suzanne Williams who I realise must have been tearing their hair out at various points when asked to clear another small ad for a watering can, or a web page that had seemingly vanished.

There are many others who have helped to create this book in the form you see and should be thanked, although I have not had contact with them individually. The design team in particular have managed to express the actuality of some of these texts and give the sense of language being used in a living context.

Thanks to my husband, Kieron O'Hara, for insisting that I stop working at various points.

All these, and many others, should be thanked for their support, insights, corrections and comments. Any remaining shortcomings should lie at my door.

The author and publishers are grateful to the following for permission to reproduce copyright material. It has not always been possible to identify the source of material used or to contact the copyright holders and in such cases the publishers would welcome information from the copyright owners.

The instructor college (www.theinstructorcollege.co.uk) for the text on p.34 from their advertisement; Frances Bissell for the recipe on p.36 from *The Times Book of Vegetarian Cookery* by Frances Bissell © Frances Bissell 1994; Extract from *Delia's Complete Cookery Course* by Delia Smith on p.37 reproduced with the permission of BBC Worldwide Limited. Copyright © Delia Smith 1978; Tesoro Electronics Inc for the extract on p.54 from the Bandido II µMax manual; Mamas and Papas Ltd for text and diagrams on p.57 taken from the Primo Viaggio Infant Carrier Instructions; Warner Books for the text on p.67 from the cover of *Plum Island* by Nelson DeMille © Time Warner 1998; extract on p.79, reproduced with permission from *Britain 3*, © 1999 Lonely Planet Publications; Sony Ericsson for the extract on p.98 from the T630 mobile phone manual; The Boots Company PLC for the text on p.109 taken from the instructions on a packet of Boots paracetamol caplets.

Illustrations by Mark Duffin pp 47

Commissioned photography by MM Studios pp 48, 51br, 95r, 107

Photographic Acknowledgements
(top = t, bottom = b, left = l, right = r, centre =c)

(credit to come from CUP for 2 photos on page 54)

Alamy pp 73tl (Neil Setchfield), 73br (Coston Stock), 77 (Travel-Shots), 79 (David Copeman), 82 (Dallas and John Heaton/ SCPhotos), 102 (Acestock Limited), 124b (Mediacolor's); Corbis pp 71 (© Close Murray), 73tr (Bob Krist), 73bl (Charles Lenars), 73bc (Owen Franken), 83 (Charles Lenars), 84b (Chris Hellier), 124t (Ludovic Maisant); Geoff Holdsworth p113; Getty Images pp 61 (Getty Images), 76 (Walter Hodges), 85b (Louis B Wallach Inc), 90 (Ken Chernus), 95l (Archive Holdings Inc), 104 (Bob Torrez), 114 (Kerrick James Photog), 124c (Lester Lefkowitz); Lonely Planet Images p 84t (John Borthwick); Photolibrary.com pp 37 (Jonelle Weaver), 51cl (Picture Plain), 88 (MarkBarrett), 115 (Brian Hagiwara); PRshots/Accessorize p 51t; Punchstock pp 65 (Comstock Images), 84c (Image100), 85t (PhotoDisc Green/Hoby Finn), 85cr (Thinkstock/Ron Chapple); Science Photo Library p 123 (TEK Image)

Photographs supplied by Pictureresearch.co.uk

Typeface Utopia 9.5/13pt   *System* QuarkXPress® [KAMAE]

Introduction

Philosophy

Why not what

This book aims to provide students with insights about the interplay of language, texts and audience. Grammar is presented as a tool for living communication between writers and readers. Grammar in writing is about communicating ideas appropriately to different audiences and understanding their needs: it is living grammar. Using largely real examples from a wide range of contexts, the book challenges the learner to ask *why* the writer chose a structure, rather than simply analyse *what* the writer used.

Factors influencing grammar and style

Rather than thinking of written language in the abstract, the book analyses the impact of the following types of factor on grammar and style:

- whether something is written to be kept as a record or written to be thrown away (*Unit 1: Everyday notes* or *Unit 17: Packaging* versus *Unit 4: Policies and agreements* or *Unit 10: Encyclopaedias*)
- whether the writer is writing for an anonymous, global readership or for a close personal friend (*Unit 16: Newspaper stories* or *Unit 18: Advertisements* versus *Unit 2: Greetings cards* or *Unit 7: Informal letters and e-mails*)
- whether the text is written primarily to inform or instruct or for a very different function (*Unit 6: Hobby Books* or *Unit 9: Technical Manuals* versus *Unit 8: Catalogues* or *Unit 14: Direct Mail*)

In each unit these contextual and functional factors are related to one or two typical language features which the texts tend to show. For instance, because newspaper stories are interested in the where, when, who, what and why of an event, they will usually be rich in adverb phrases locating and explaining circumstances. These stories are limited in terms of space, and so they will also contain devices to shorten the message, for example specific prepositional phrases used as a shorthand for longer clauses. Crucially, this book aims to link easily grasped real-world writing constraints and influencing factors with an explanation of the grammar featured in these same contexts.

Approach

An inductive, awareness-raising approach informs the book. Clear summaries reinforce key points, but the tasks themselves first ask the student to think about why a structure or word choice has been made in that particular context. This is particularly clear in the *Think about why* tasks, but the majority of the material is written with this questioning approach in mind.

The book is intended to have features which appeal to both analytical and more communication focused learners. Standard grammatical terms are used as far as possible, and any terms which may be unfamiliar or need revision are in the glossary. Many of the tasks ask the student to locate and analyse a particular grammatical structure in context. However, the tasks are also intended to move beyond these sentence level insights, to encourage debate over why one form has been used over another.

Level

The tasks are designed to be carried out by students at upper-intermediate or advanced levels. It is assumed that the student has a productive writing skill around a strong 5.0 in IELTS and a reading ability slightly above this. However, the combination of work on accuracy and on style and register means that this is also excellent supplementary material for higher level students, including those on CAE or CPE courses.

The data

This book is based on a broad cross-section of authentic material written in English. The data for the book are taken from a wide variety of texts, and are in many cases from the Cambridge International Corpus.

New technologies are challenging our conception of texts as the process of writing takes place more and more within the context of electronic media. In addition to more familiar types of writing, such as letters and published texts, this book examines the influence of the medium of production on some of the newer genres of writing that are emerging (for example, e-mail messages or internet pages).

The book incorporates some of the more ephemeral and marginal types of writing which are produced in English, such as notes and cards. These texts are of particular interest for an advanced learner of English, since they are genres which can be very challenging to produce but which are in everyday use.

The design of the units

The material is designed for both class and self-study use. Each unit follows the same pattern and deals with one broad category of texts. Section A provides an example of the text type along with an opening task which asks the student to relate a main idea from the unit to their own life experience. This can be used in class for a warm-up phase, or to orient the self-study user. The opening section ends with a *Think about why* task which prompts the student to think about a key feature of the text type and relate this to a language point.

Section B provides the main language points of the unit, presented in the context of the text types in question. The tasks here are intended to be awareness-raising and provoke some discussion. Summary boxes draw together the language points raised. Students are given the opportunity to practise items in section C. In some cases students may need to return to section B and review the summaries in the light of the more productive tasks. In section D there are follow-up tasks which are designed as mini language awareness projects on the topics being discussed or for more extended writing practice.

The tasks in sections A, B and C have clear answers which are provided in the key, but the successful use of the book does not only lie in getting through the material efficiently and checking your answers are right. In teaching from these materials, it is the discussion generated by prompts for thinking about why which provides the most meaningful language learning experiences.

PART 1

Writing for different readers

Everyday notes

A Introduction

1 ● When do people need to write notes to other people?

● Are there any circumstances when you would write a note to a complete stranger? Would this be very different from a note to a friend? ☜

2 Match the notes with the following places where they were found: kitchen door, inside front door, printer, manuscript, desk. ☜

a) Move this to Rm A12d too. Thanks, Peter Evans

b) Milk

c) Here's the first draft – mostly as agreed – some changes to pp. 10-12. Cheers, Charlie

d) Tina rang (finally!) – arriving for the meeting Friday. Will e-mail re arrival time. Believe it when I see it!! S

e) Broke a glass. Take care! Love (me) xxxx

● Put H next to ones written at home and W next to ones from work. Why were they written?

Think about why ☜

Most people do not keep day-to-day notes. They are written quickly, and they are usually thrown away when they have been read. How does this affect the language people use when they write a note?

B Language working in context 🔑

1 Shortening the message by using ellipsis

a) In some of the following the writer has left out words to make the sentences suitable for a note. Mark these sentences with a cross.

1 Rang Peter. (*X*)

2 Might be back around 7. (*X*)

3 Please ring Peter.

4 Mo'hd sending the files on Friday. (*X*)

5 Am leaving tonight. (*X*)

6 Will e-mail my arrival time. (*X*)

7 Couldn't find keys. Taken yours. (*X*)

8 John e-mailed the details.

9 Transfers from airport arranged with Michael Evans. (*X*)

b) Write out a longer version of each clause where there is ellipsis. What part of the sentence has been left out?

Rang Peter

→ I rang Peter. (The subject has been left out.)

....

....

....

....

....

....

c) Compare the two versions you have produced and answer the following questions:

1 Can you omit first person pronouns in notes?

2 Can you omit the auxiliary verbs *be* and *have*?

3 Can you omit modal auxiliaries?

Think about why 🔑

Will notes to friends and family be different from notes to work colleagues or acquaintances?

Summary

Notes naturally contain the minimum words for the message to be clear. This process is called ellipsis. You can leave out more words if you are sure the reader will understand.

● You can generally leave out first person pronouns to reduce the length of a message:

(I) rang Joan.

● It is also common to remove auxiliary verbs *be* and *have*:

Joan (is) leaving on Friday.
Meeting (has) (been) cancelled.

● The writer can also choose to omit both auxiliary verbs and first person pronouns, but care is needed so that the meaning remains clear:

(I) (have) been sick again. (I) (have) gone home.

● You cannot leave out modal auxiliary verbs, since omitting them will always change the meaning:

(I) might ring later. (I) can't ring later.

2 Common abbreviations and when to use them

a) Look at these notes. What do the abbreviations mean?

1 Will send dets asap.

   dets = details, asap = as soon as possible

2 Parcel due Fri a.m.

   ....

3 Can you ring Joan on 020 678932 ext. 143?

   ....

4 John gave wrong fax no.

   ....

5 Here are the figs for the last quarter (ie Oct to Jan).

   ....

6 Could you bring some sample docs? (e.g. the yellow brochures)

   ....

7 NB the alarm is set!

   ....

8 P.S. I love you!

   ....

b) **Abbreviations are frequently used in text messages, too. Can you translate these messages?**

1 CU ....

2 CU2NITE ....

3 CUL8R ....

4 WAN2CU ....

5 GR8 ....

6 RUOK? ....

7 YRUL8? ....

8 NE MSG? ....

9 XLNT ....

10 RNG B4 U GO ....

Summary

There are a number of conventional abbreviations in English. These, and contracted verb forms are often used in informal notes.

- Punctuation is used to show shortening and abbreviation (full stops, dashes, apostrophes), but is not essential.

- Abbreviations are based on spelling, sound or the first letters of a group of words:

  facsimile ➛ *fax*
  extension ➛ *X*
  before ➛ *B4*
  estimated time of arrival ➛ *eta*

- Many abbreviations which are useful in everyday notes are originally from Latin:

N.B. (nota bene)	remember
e.g. (exampli gratia)	for example
a.m. (ante meridiem)	before noon = morning
p.m. (post meridiem)	after noon = afternoon
i.e. (id est)	that is
P.S. (postscriptum)	after writing
etc. (et cetera)	and the other

- A good dictionary will often list the accepted abbreviations of common words.

C Language practice 🔑

1 **Look at these notes and correct any mistakes.**

a) I posting report Mon

Am posting report Mon

b) I finishing first draft today

c) Am 2 tired

d) Can't meet Henry 2nite

e) John ring

f) I not read your writing!

g) Not going to the party

h) Sally has delayed. Will start the meeting on my own.

i) Didn't bring the car

2 **Here are some commonly abbreviated words. How would you shorten them in a note?**

a) because ....
b) between ....
c) birthday ....
d) Christmas ....
e) committee ....
f) enclosed ....
g) forward ....

h) information ....
i) month ....
j) number ....
k) possible ....
l) telephone ....
m) weekend ....
n) your ....

3 Rewrite these notes with abbreviations in the appropriate places.

a) Please include comparative sales figures for another area, for example: Northern branches.

→ *Pls inc comparative sales figs for another area, e.g. Northern branches.*

b) Will have report regarding the tax situation by Wednesday.

....

c) Remember: Read this before the meeting!

....

d) Will send the information as soon as possible.

....

e) There has been a power cut all afternoon. That's to say, I could not make the dinner. Let us eat out!

....

....

f) There have been three urgent facsimile messages.

....

D Follow-up tasks

1 **Imagine you are writing a note to give someone a telephone message. The message is that the caller wants your flatmate to contact them later, but will be out from 2 to 3 in the afternoon.**

  ● **What information would you include? Write the note.** 🔑

2 **Here is a list of unlikely, but real, excuses given by people for not arriving at work on time.**

  ● **Choose one of these and write a note to a friend at work explaining what has happened, and asking them to tell the boss!**

a) being questioned by the FBI

b) being abducted by aliens

c) having problems with the alarm clock because the cat sat on it

d) having your keys buried by the dog

e) running over a rabbit

Conventional expressions used for different occasions

Varying the warmth and formality of the message

A Introduction

1 ● On what occasions do you send someone a greetings card? Have you ever sent a greetings card to someone in English?

● Are there standard expressions in your language for special days and events?

2 Decide which of the cards relates to the following: an illness, passing an exam, a retirement. ⌁

a)

b)

Get Well Soon

All the Very Best for the Future

Congratulations!

c)

Think about why ⌁

In many cases you can buy greetings cards with the message already printed by the publisher. Why is this possible?

B Language working in context ⌐

1 Conventional expressions used for different occasions

a) Look at this list of expressions from cards. Decide what event they relate to.

1 Compliments of the season
2 Birthday wishes
3 Happy anniversary!
4 Sincere condolences
5 Congratulations!
6 Happy New Year!
7 Get well soon!
8 Many happy returns!
9 Merry Xmas!
10 Belated birthday greetings

Think about why ⌐

What effect does leaving out words have? Why are shortened messages not always appropriate?

Summary

Expressions that relate to special occasions are often fixed, e.g. *Season's greetings* (Christmas), *Many happy returns* (birthday). Writers cannot vary these and sometimes the greeting is already printed on the card when you buy it.

The nouns which express the message are generally plural, e.g. *wishes*, *greetings*, *congratulations*, *condolences*, and cannot be made singular.

This is also true of the more general expressions *Best wishes* and *Regards*.

b) Make as many correct sentences as you can.

1 I hope …   … you are well.
2 Wishing …   … you a speedy recovery.
3 Hoping …   … you were here.
4 Best …   … to see you soon.
5 I wish …   … all is going well.
6 Hope …   … wishes.

Summary

The words *wish* and *hope* are used very commonly in greetings cards in ways that are conventionalised.

● *Wish* is used both as a verb, generally in the participle form, or as a plural noun:

Wishing you every happiness, Best wishes.

● *Hope* is found mainly in the following constructions:

I/We hope + clause, e.g. *I hope (that) all is well.*
Hoping to + clause, e.g. *Hoping to see you soon.*
Hoping + clause, e.g. *Hoping all is well.*

2 Varying the warmth and formality of the message

a) **Look at this list of ways to close a message. Which ones are not suitable for cards because they are too formal? Mark them F for formal.**

1	Best wishes	7	Regards
2	Love	8	Thinking of you
3	Much love	9	Yours faithfully
4	Lots of love	10	Kind regards
5	Yours sincerely	11	Yours truly
6	Love from us all	12	With all my love

b) **Mark the remaining expressions N (neutrally friendly), W (warm), X (only for close friends and family).**

c) **How many words can you remove from the following sentences and retain the meaning?**

1 I hope that you are well.
   → Hope you're well.
   ....

2 I hope to see you soon.
   ....

3 Wishing you every happiness.
   ....

4 Please accept my sincere best wishes.
   ....

5 I am sending congratulations on behalf of all the team.
   ....

6 I am writing to send my sincere condolences on your loss.
   ....

d) Here are two examples of online greetings cards. Decide what is wrong with the message in each case.

1

Darling
I am writing to wish you sincere congratulations
Yours sincerely, Rebecca

2

Sometimes the hurt is too big for words.

Hi!
Thinking of you!!
Love
Rebecca

Summary

Several things work together to change the level of formality and warmth in a greetings card, such as the choice of ways to close a message or leaving out words.

- The more words which are left out from sentences on cards, the more informal and direct the style:

  I hope to see you soon. → *See you soon.*

  Care is needed when the greetings card relates to a serious event, such as illness or bereavement, as an informal style may seem too casual:

  I am writing to send my sincere condolences on your loss.
  → *Sincere condolences on your loss* ✓
  → ~~Condolences on your loss~~ ✗
  → ~~Condolences~~ ✗

- Using non-standard punctuation, e.g. exclamation marks or doubled question marks, can also help to make messages seem informal and friendly.

  Excellent news!!

C Language practice 🔑

1 Match the descriptions to the cards.

a) This is a birthday card from a close friend.

b) This is from the colleague of someone who is leaving their job.

c) This is a birthday card from an aunt to her niece.

d) This is a birthday card from a close friend that is three days late!

e) This is from friends of a couple who are getting married.

i)
Wishing you a very happy
birthday
With love and best wishes
from
Sally and family

iv)
Never mind darling –
it'll be worse next year ...
Lots of love
Lucy XXX[1]

ii)
Congratulations on your
new job.
All the very best for
the future.
Kind regards
Eddie (Mather)

v)
Good luck on the big day!
Love
Ann and John

iii)
Sorry!! Hope you had a great time!
Lots of love
Suzy X

2 Choose the correct form of *wish* or *hope*.

a) *To wishing/Wishing* you a Happy New Year.

b) *Wishing/Hoping* to see you soon.

c) *Hoping to/Hope* you are better.

d) *Wish/To wish* you were here.

e) I *wish/hope* you have a lovely day.

---

[1] X is used to mean a kiss

3 Look at these conventional expressions and correct any mistakes.

a) Good Christmas!

b) Merry New Year!

c) Be well soon!

d) Best wishes

e) Happy Anniversary!

f) Good lucks!

g) Many happy birthdays!

h) Congratulation!

4 Choose one of the following contexts and write an appropriate message.

- birthday card to a work colleague

- get well card to a close friend

- retirement card to your boss

D Follow-up tasks

1 Collect as many examples of greetings cards as you can (in any language). Make a list of the fixed expressions you find.

- If the cards are in English, did you find any new expressions?

- If they are in another language, are the expressions similarly fixed, or are they more flexible?

2 Using the same cards you collected for the previous task, make a list of the expressions under the headings: *neutral to friendly* and *friendly to very friendly*.

- Translate some of the expressions into English or into your own language. Discuss the translations with another speaker of the language and see if they agree!

3 Formal letters and e-mails

Expressing requests for action and making suggestions

Combining conditionals and modals to make requests

(A) Introduction

1 Have you received a letter or an e-mail from a company or organisation recently? What was the letter about? Did the letter ask you to do something?

2 Look at this business e-mail.

● What type of business is it? What is it asking the reader to do? 🔑

Send Now | Send Later | Save as Draft | Add Attachments | Signature ▾ | Options ▾ | Rewrap

▷ Attachments: *none*

Default Font ▾ | Text Size ▾ | **B** *I* U T | ≡ ≡ ≡ | ≔ ≔ ≔ | A ▾ · ◇ ▾ | —

Dear Ms Hughes

Updated information has been recorded for new property in the following area(s):

West Bridgford, NG2

Log in with your username and password at
http://web.estate4u.com

We have also recently improved our service in several ways, including virtual property tours. If you wish to benefit from these, please log in and select the 'silver service' option. We would be grateful if you could take a moment to re-confirm your personal profile at the same time.

Regards,
The Estate4U customer service

Think about why 🔑

Which part of the e-mail is most formal and polite? Why does the style change like this?

B Language working in context ⚏

1 Expressing requests for action and making suggestions

a) Look at the following text. Why was it written? Is it possible to guess what the original query was?

```
○ ○ ○                          New Message                              ⬭

 ✈     💬     📎     @     A     ⬤     🗎
Send  Chat  Attach  Address  Fonts  Colors  Save As Draft

   To:  r.brown@newworld.com

   Cc:

Subject:  Your query – 0069714

   A personal response from one of our staff will be sent to you soon but if you
   need to contact us about your original message, please quote the tracking
   number above which will help us to assist you more quickly.

   As a BC credit card customer you may have heard of some of the other
   services that we offer. If you would like to know more, please click on the link
   given below.

                                                          ( more info )
```

b) Look at the underlined clauses. What are they examples of? Why does the writer need to use them?

Summary

- Writers of formal letters may need to request an action by the reader. Conditional clauses are useful because they allow the writer to make a request that will fit a number of different circumstances:

  If you have already paid this bill, please ignore this letter. (Phrased in this way in case the reader is offended by the request for late payment.)

- Conditional sentences are also used to encourage readers to do a wide range of things which the business or organisation wants:

  If you have not yet used all your tax allowance for the year, let us know and we can recommend further investment opportunities. (The writer wants to do more business with the customer and makes a suggestion of something the reader might want to do.)

c) **What are these extracts about? Underline the requests for action.**

1

Thank you for your e-mail. Please change your reservation as soon as possible. If you wait until the day of travel, you will have less chance of obtaining a place on the later sailing.

2

Please contact me urgently on 0124 347767 concerning your account. Alternatively if outside normal office hours contact Customer Care on the above number, which offers a 6am to 9pm service.

3

Thank you for your kind enquiry. We have one room left on 28th August with en-suite shower and sea view. The rate is £86.00 inclusive of breakfast.

If you could give us a credit card number, we will reserve the room for you.

Think about why ☞

In the third extract above the writer uses a conditional form. Change this into a direct request using an imperative form. How does this change the effect?

Summary

Writers need to be able to vary their style to suit the request.

- Imperatives are used when the action by the reader is expected or understood:

  Thank you for your request for an application pack. Please complete the enclosed and return by the closing date. (The action by the reader is expected, because they have asked for the application pack.)

- Actions which the writer can demand from the reader are also expressed as a simple imperative:

  Please telephone your account manager to discuss the lack of funds in your account. (The writer does not need to soften this, because the reader is in the wrong!)

  Both uses of the imperative are generally preceded by *please*.

- Actions which are more difficult or are unexpected are requested through conditional forms and modal verbs. They are built around a basic imperative clause:

  Please e-mail us, and we will send your password.
  ➤ *If you e-mail us, we will send your password.*
  ➤ *If you could e-mail us, we will send your password.*

2 Combining conditionals and modals to make requests

a) **Match the statements to the actions that are requested.**

1 If you could sign the enclosed contract, we will complete the necessary arrangements.

2 We would be glad to send further information if you could confirm your contact details.

3 We would be very grateful if you could complete the attached questionnaire. It should not take more than 20 minutes.

4 If you could possibly ask your friends to take part too, we will send you some additional sponsorship forms.

5 If you are having problems, please read the FAQ page on our website first.

6 We would be extremely grateful if you could enclose two passport-sized photographs with your signature on the back.

a) Don't e-mail us!

b) Send your address.

c) Fill in a form.

d) Add your signature to a legal document.

e) Find more people to help a charity.

f) Send evidence of your identity.

b) **Which are the easiest actions for the reader and which are the most difficult? How is this reflected in the language?**

Summary

- In English direct instructions are often avoided because they can be considered rude. The form *If you could …* is a very common polite form of request for an action by the reader.

- Requests for difficult actions are preceded or followed by conventional forms such as *we would be (very / most / extremely) grateful, we would be glad, we would be pleased, if you could possibly*:

  We would be extremely grateful if you could send us your passport number.
  If you could possibly make an appointment next week, we would be grateful.

C Language practice ⚷

1 **You work for an online bank. You have made the following notes on some possible customer problems. Write an appropriate request for these actions so that a standard e-mail can be sent to every customer.**

customer enquiry:	action:
a) customer requires more information	fill in details below
b) customer wants free virus protection software	download from our website
c) customer receives request for account details and password	ignore and contact us immediately
d) customer wants to know when the new account is ready for use	send a daytime contact number or e-mail address, we will confirm when the new account is 'live'

a) ....

b) ....

c) ....

d) ....

2

a) **Mark these requests for customer action. Put ! for difficult or unexpected requests or ✓ for easy or expected requests.**

1 telephone us urgently

2 complete the enclosed form (customer requested it)

3 pay a bill within 10 days (customer has already received reminder)

4 send in some documents to confirm customer's identity

5 click on a link and it will automatically update the security settings

6 send passport and a separate photograph

b) **Choose two easy and two difficult requests and write them in an appropriate style.**

3 You work for an airline company. You have been told to contact customers in the Fly4fun club by e-mail. You have made the following notes about what you need to say to the customers. Write the complete e-mail.

Ask customers to
- re-register on the website
- change their security settings at the same time (follow simple instructions)

Suggest
- might be interested in further info on special promotions

Start like this:
Packed with lots of exciting new features, the Fly4fun website is even better than before! Just give us a couple of minutes of your time and you could access a great new world of offers ...

D Follow-up tasks

1 Think of a situation when you need to write a formal letter or e-mail requesting an action.

- Make notes on the key information to include.
- If you are working in class, give the notes to a classmate and ask them to write the letter or e-mail.

2 Collect as many letters from organisations to individuals as you can (in any language).

- If these are in English, do they contain any of the features worked on in this unit?
- If these are in your own language, analyse whether the language varies according to the action being requested. Is the language more formal and polite when something difficult is being requested? What forms are used?

UNIT 4

Policies and agreements

Modals and semi-modals of obligation

Formal versus informal language choices

Ⓐ Introduction

1 ● **Look at these different kinds of policy and agreement. Can you think of any others?**

*travel insurance, guarantee, software licence, buildings insurance,
health insurance, extended warranty[1], car insurance*

● **Are any of the above obligatory? For example, in the UK it is illegal to drive without car insurance.** ○⇌

2 **Look at this extract from an insurance policy.**

● **Underline the modal forms. Which one expresses obligation?** ○⇌

> **Conditions**
>
> An insured person must:
> - adhere to the terms and conditions of this policy.
> - take reasonable steps to restrict amounts we are obliged to pay.
> - endeavour to prevent occurrences that might cause a claim.

● **Find synonyms for the words *try* and *keep*.**

Think about why ○⇌

Why are synonyms for *try* and *keep* used in this context? Why do writers feel they have to use special language for policies and agreements?

---

[1] An *extended warranty* is a guarantee that you can buy. It adds time to the normal guarantee, for example, a further year.

1 Modals and semi-modals of obligation

a) **Read this extract from a home insurance policy. Which modal verbs are used to express strong obligation?**

> All previous losses, potential claims and convictions should be fully declared on your insurance application. ... You have a responsibility to check the accuracy of any application forms completed and you must ensure that any information you may have given us verbally or in writing relevant to your application has been stated on the form.
>
> It is your responsibility to check the policy documents received and ensure that the cover provided meets absolutely with your requirements. You must do this immediately upon receiving your documents and if the insurance cover is not exactly as you had intended then you must contact us within three working days to enable us to replace your cover.

b) **Could you replace any of the modal verbs with *have to*?**

Summary

There are several modal verbs and semi-modal verbs of obligation used in policies, agreements and guarantees.

- *Must* and *should* are standard modals and are both used to tell a reader they have no choice about an action. *Must* is stronger than *should*.

  Your application must include a photograph.

- The semi-modal *have to* and, less frequently, *need to* also express mandatory actions. *Have to* is slightly stronger than *need to*. They are both less formal than *must* and *should*:

  You have to pay taxes.
  You need to get tax advice when you move to a new country.

2 Formal versus informal language choices

a) **Which of the following examples were found in real guarantees or insurance policies?**

1   In the unlikely event that a fault should occur, to claim under this guarantee return the item to Mason (UK) Ltd, together with the receipt.

2   If a fault happens, you can claim under this guarantee by returning this pan to Mason (UK) Ltd, with the receipt.

3 If you stop paying premiums[1] on the policy and we have to refund the commissions[2] paid to us because of this, we have a right to charge you a fee …

4 If you subsequently cease to pay premiums on the policy, and in consequence, we are obliged to refund the commissions paid to us, we reserve the right to charge you a fee …

b) Underline the words or phrases in the extracts which are particularly formal.

Summary

There are a number of ways in which legal documents are made to sound authoritative:

- Prepositional phrases in place of single words:

in the (unlikely) event that	if
on expiry of	after
in respect of	about
in consequence	so
in excess of	more than

- Longer, more formal word choice (often of Latin or Greek origin):

modification	change
provided that	if
defect	fault or problem
cease or terminate	stop
commence	start
exceeding	more than

You can recognise words of Latin origin because they often start with a prefix such as: *ad-, co-, in-, inter-, pre-, re-, semi-* or *trans-*.

Words with Greek origin also begin with recognisable prefixes such as: *auto-, geo-, hydro-, mono-, theo-*.

- The use of *should* to express a condition (subjunctive use, rather than modal form) is also particularly formal. It is used in two patterns:

If the contract should be terminated within six months, no further claims can be made.
Should the contract be terminated within six months, no further claims can be made.

---

[1] A *premium* is a fee paid to an insurer, monthly or annually.

[2] *Commission* is the money paid by an insurer to a dealer or broker.

c) **Read this extract from an agreement between an internet service provider and customers. Find phrases with the verb *be* which mean the same as *must* or *must not*.**

Live Home Page   Apple   iTools   Apple Support   Apple Store   Microsoft MacTopia   MSN   Office for Macintosh   Internet Explorer

Favorites History Search Scrapbook Page Holder

All new customers are required to submit a signed copy of the applicable Server and Domain Registration Agreements.

Accounts still outstanding on the last day of the month are subject to immediate termination.

You are prohibited from sending unsolicited bulk mail messages ("junk mail" or "spam").

Virtual Servers which use CPU processing capacity on the Physical Server in excess of the designed processing capacity will be subject to immediate deactivation.

Summary

- A number of semi-modal verbs expressing obligation or prohibition are in the form of *be* + (past participle or adjective) + *to*:

be +	not allowed expected obliged required subject supposed	+ *to* + infinitive

You are required to sign and return the form within 7 days.

- Two semi-modals expressing prohibition take the pattern: *be* + past participle + *from*:

be +	banned prohibited	+ *from* + –*ing* form

You are prohibited from leaving the country.

Think about why 🔑

Because the *be* forms in the Summary box are either passives or contain adjectives the writer does not have to state who requires or expects the action. Why is this useful?

C Language practice 🔑

1 Rewrite each of these sentences using one of the following modal forms:
should (not), must (not), need to, need not, have to, do not have to.

a) The company rules do not allow you to take money out of the country.

→ *You must not take money out of the country.*

b) The company does not expect you to sign until you have legal advice.

....

c) The insurer does not recommend that you lend your car to another driver.

....

d) The company requires you to sign by the end of the month.

....

e) The insurer advises strongly that you let them know if you change job.

....

f) The company prohibits you from holding a non-European account.

....

2 Find words in these extracts which mean the same as *after* and *if (×2)*.

a) You may cancel this agreement within 7 days, provided that no claim has been made and the service has not been used during the current policy period.

b) On expiry of the 90 days, you will not be entitled to a refund.

c) In the event that the products fail to meet the required standard, please return to the address indicated below.

3 Match these words to their more formal equivalents.

a)	change (noun)	i)	commencement
b)	for (+ someone)	ii)	subsequent to
c)	beginning	iii)	deficiency
d)	after	iv)	exclusion
e)	lack of something	v)	in case of
f)	if	vi)	modification
g)	end (noun)	vii)	exceeding
h)	something left out	viii)	on behalf of
i)	more than	ix)	termination

4

a) **Read this extract from a guarantee and answer the questions.**

> During the subsequent four years after purchase, any defective
> parts will be replaced free – labour costs only being chargeable –
> provided that the Guarantee Registration card is returned to the
> Company within 14 days of the purchase.

1   What happens if I return the guarantee registration card 15 days after
    buying the item?
2   Will they help me more than four years after I bought the item?
3   Will I have to pay for repair work if I have a valid guarantee?
4   And will I have to pay for the parts?

b) **If you are working in class, write a simple summary of the extract. Give it to a
classmate and ask them to rewrite it in a more formal style. Compare their
version with the original.**

D Follow-up tasks

1   Imagine that you are setting up a boat-hire firm at the seaside. Make a list of
    rules and advice for the people who are taking the boats. Are you going to ask
    them for a deposit? Is it necessary for all the passengers to be able to swim? ⚷

    ● Write an agreement for them to sign before they take a boat. Remember,
    anything you forget to put in may mean you get into trouble or lose
    money!

2   Next time you are using a computer, look at the licence agreement for the
    software installed on the machine.

    ● Make a list of the modals of obligation and semi-modals with similar
    meaning. Does the text contain any of the formal words and phrases listed
    in this unit? Can you add to the list?

PART 2

Building noun phrases

Patterns of noun phrases

Writing opening statements

A Introduction

1 ● When do you need to write a formal letter to a business or other organisation? ⚷

● Have you ever had to write a business letter in English?

2 What is the main purpose of this letter? ⚷

Dear Mr Smith

Re: reference for Mrs Saskia Ferrer

I write in response to your request for a reference for Mrs Saskia Ferrer. Mrs Ferrer has worked as my secretary for the last three years, and has been an excellent employee. She has carried out her work with energy, enthusiasm and efficiency.

I believe that she meets all the requirements mentioned in your job description, and indeed exceeds these in many ways. She has, for example, taken confidential meeting notes and minutes for many years and I have never had reason to doubt her complete integrity.

I would, therefore, recommend Mrs Ferrer for the post you advertise.

Yours sincerely,

John Taylor

Professor John Taylor

Think about why ⚷

Look at the line in bold in the sample letter. Why is this used?

1 Patterns of noun phrases

a) Put the following letter back into the correct order.

1 I wish to reject the goods and claim a refund. Please respond to my complaint within seven days.

2 Dear Sir/Madam,

3 **Re: problem with a fridge-freezer**

4 Yours faithfully,

5 I am writing to complain about the fridge-freezer which I bought from your store.

6 Angela Hardy

7 On 20th February, I bought a Gold Star fridge-freezer from you for £750. This machine is faulty as the handle on the freezer has broken.

b) Underline any noun phrases that have more than two words. One has already been done.

c) Match the underlined phrases to the following patterns:
noun + prepositional phrase
noun + clause

Think about why ⌒

Writers can choose to add information either before or after the main noun. Information in front of the noun usually gives descriptive details and can show the opinion of the writer. Information after the noun often gives more factual details. Which type will be most common in formal business letters?

Summary

● A basic noun phrase is a main noun and any other words that are linked to it in a unit:

beautiful <u>day</u> (adjective + noun = noun phrase)
a beautiful <u>day</u> for a picnic (article + adjective + noun + prepositional phrase = noun phrase)

● Writers often choose to put information after the noun in formal, information-focused writing. There are two typical ways you can add information after a main noun:

the <u>beginning</u> of the 20th century (noun + phrase)
the <u>job</u> which was advertised in 'The Times' (noun + clause)

d) **Who are these letters to? Match the topic statements to the following recipients: estate agent, property landlord, family lawyer (×3), an organisation with a job vacancy (×2).**

1   Re: Start of divorce proceedings   *To family lawyer* ....

2   Re: Late payment of rent

3   Re: Further particulars of 19 Lovedale Road

4   Re: Draft will in name of Mr H Sayed

5   Re: Claim for compensation on behalf of Mrs J Jones

6   Re: Request for further details and application form

7   Re: Further information about the post of headteacher at Margrave School

e) **Identify the main noun in each example and the prepositional phrase that goes with it.**

1   *start (main noun), of divorce proceedings (prep phrase)* ....

2   ....

3   ....

4   ....

5   ....

6   ....

7   ....

Summary

A noun phrase is used to express the main idea in business letters. This is often placed in a single line below the opening greeting, and is preceded by *Re:* (= on the subject of). The words are often in bold, or underlined.

Re: Repair of washing machine.

In this context the noun phrases omit the standard articles:

✗ Re: ~~The~~ cancellation of ~~an~~ agreement
✓ Re: Cancellation of agreement

These noun phrases can also be used as the subject line in a business e-mail.

2 Writing opening statements

a) What form of the word in brackets would you use to complete the opening statements of these letters?

1

> **Re: Estimate for repairs to roof**
>
> I am writing .... (request) an estimate for the repair of storm damage to my roof to give to my insurers.

2

> **Re: Insurance claim ref. 00098/HM**
>
> I am writing .... (regard) the above claim.

b) Which opening statement is about an action?

Summary

It is normal to begin the first main paragraph of a business letter with an explicit statement about why you are writing the letter. Opening statements need to be very clear, and they follow certain fixed patterns.

- If you want to express your main topic using a verb, the structure is *I am writing* + *to* + infinitive:

  I am writing <u>to enquire</u> about the vacancy for a sales manager.

- If you want to express your main topic using a noun, the form is *I am writing* + *with regard to / regarding / about* + noun phrase:

  I am writing regarding the vacancy for a sales manager.

  With regard to is the most formal and *about* is the least formal.

- *I write* can replace *I am writing* in either type of sentence, making the style formal and a little old fashioned:

  I write to suggest / suggesting that there has been an error in my recent telephone bill.

1 Rewrite the following business letter topics using the appropriate noun phrase.

a) I want to ask about an insurance policy, number 678-987-HP.

→ *Re: Policy no.678-978-HP*

b) I want some job details. The reference number is PG/107/B.

c) I want to find out more about an application procedure.

d) I want to ask about an invoice. The number is 1009/8.

e) I have a question about a tenancy agreement for Flat 4, 76 Park Road.

f) I want to find out why I haven't had a reply to a letter of complaint.

2

a) Write the opening sentence to a letter on each of the six topics in the previous activity. Use each of these sentence patterns.

1 I am writing + to + infinitive

→ *I am writing to request further job details.*

2 I am writing + regarding + noun phrase

3 I write + to + infinitive

4 I am writing + with regard to + noun phrase

5 I am writing + about + noun phrase

6 I write + regarding + noun phrase

b) Decide if the patterns you have chosen are neutral, more formal or less formal. Mark them N, MF or LF.

3 Look at the following advertisement. Write an e-mail requesting further information and an application form.

Become a
Driving Instructor
with The Instructor College

Earn around £500–£600 per week
with a guaranteed position and a fully maintained car

flexible working hours
choose when and where you operate after flexible training period

No previous qualification necessary*
you must have held a car licence for min. 3½ years

Ref: TX771

Freephone
0500 170017
www.theinstructorcollege.co.uk

D Follow-up tasks

1 Collect as many examples of business letters as you can.

- Underline the main topic statement, and the opening sentence in each one. Are the topic statements all noun phrases? Do the opening sentences follow the patterns you have worked on in this unit?

2 Think of a situation when you need to write a formal business letter.

- Write your own letter, with a clear opening statement.

- If you are working in class, do not write in the main topic noun phrase. Ask a classmate if they can guess who the letter is to, and write in the noun phrase.

UNIT 6 Hobby books

Using articles with countable and uncountable nouns

Degree adverbs

A Introduction

1 **Do you have a hobby? Is it an activity you do inside the house or outside? Why do you like it?**

2 **Here is an extract from an online hobby course.**

- **What is the hobby?**

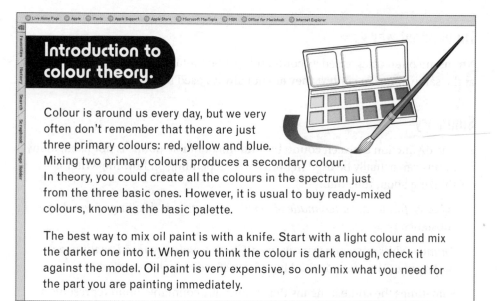

Introduction to colour theory.

Colour is around us every day, but we very often don't remember that there are just three primary colours: red, yellow and blue. Mixing two primary colours produces a secondary colour. In theory, you could create all the colours in the spectrum just from the three basic ones. However, it is usual to buy ready-mixed colours, known as the basic palette.

The best way to mix oil paint is with a knife. Start with a light colour and mix the darker one into it. When you think the colour is dark enough, check it against the model. Oil paint is very expensive, so only mix what you need for the part you are painting immediately.

- **Find adverbs in the text which mean the same as *only* and *sufficiently*.**

Think about why

Find and underline each example of the word *colour(s)*. Why is the word used as a countable noun in some examples and an uncountable noun in others?

B Language working in context ○━

1 Using articles with countable and uncountable nouns

a) **Are the following nouns countable or uncountable?**

potato   flour   dough   moisture

b) **Underline all the examples of the same nouns in this recipe. Decide whether they are being used as countable or uncountable nouns.**

Potato Gnocchi

455 g cooked mashed potato
approx. 230 g plain flour

Mix the potato and flour until you have a kneadable dough. More or less flour may be required depending on the amount of moisture in the potatoes. Knead the dough lightly ...

Think about why ○━

Nouns are often categorised as countable or uncountable. However, when you look at the same nouns in context they are not always used in this way. Why is this?

Summary

● The distinction between countable and uncountable nouns is not fixed. Many nouns can actually be used in both ways, depending on how the writer is thinking about the noun:

Window frames are often made of wood. (The writer is thinking of wood as a substance.)

Antique tables are made from many different woods: rosewood, walnut, oak, mahogany. (The writer is thinking of lots of individual woods.)

Sometimes the context means that a normally countable noun represents a concept, or a substance:

I don't eat onion.

● If a countable noun is used in front of another noun, it functions like an adjective. It gives the substance or defines the type and therefore becomes more like an uncountable noun:

a pie made from apples ➤ *an apple pie* (*apple* = substance)
a house built in a tree ➤ *a tree house* (*tree* = type)

c) Complete the gaps in the recipe using items from the ingredients list. Decide whether you need to add *the* to the nouns.

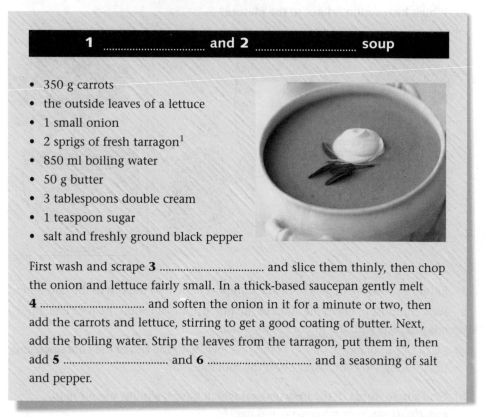

1 .... and **2** .... soup

- 350 g carrots
- the outside leaves of a lettuce
- 1 small onion
- 2 sprigs of fresh tarragon[1]
- 850 ml boiling water
- 50 g butter
- 3 tablespoons double cream
- 1 teaspoon sugar
- salt and freshly ground black pepper

First wash and scrape **3** .... and slice them thinly, then chop the onion and lettuce fairly small. In a thick-based saucepan gently melt **4** .... and soften the onion in it for a minute or two, then add the carrots and lettuce, stirring to get a good coating of butter. Next, add the boiling water. Strip the leaves from the tarragon, put them in, then add **5** .... and **6** .... and a seasoning of salt and pepper.

Summary

The countable / uncountable distinction is essential in deciding when to use articles.

- When the writer is thinking of the noun as countable, she will use *a/an* with one item, *some* with a selection, and no article to make a general statement:

  I ate <u>an apple</u> for lunch. (countable use, referring to one)
  I gave my neighbour <u>some apples</u> from my tree. (countable use, referring to a selection)
  <u>Apples</u> are supposed to be very good for you. (countable use, referring to all apples)

- When the writer is thinking of the noun as uncountable, she will use no article and the verb in singular:

  Apple is my favourite pie filling. (uncountable use, substance)

- The definite article *the* is used when a writer wants to specify a particular thing already referred to, or known to both reader and writer:

  I ate <u>the apple</u> you gave me from your tree. It was lovely.

---

[1] *Tarragon* is a herb.

2 Degree adverbs

a) Which instruction relates to the picture?

1 Fill with a mixture of good soil and compost almost to the rim of the container.

2 Pack compost in down the sides of the pot, firming it round the root ball, until it is just level with the top of the root ball.

3 Place a layer of gravel on top of the soil, level with the rim of the container, and thick enough to completely cover the root ball.

b) Find single words in the instructions which have a similar meaning to *exactly*, *as much as necessary*, and *nearly*.

Summary

Degree adverbs say how much or how far an action is to be done. They include: *almost, nearly, hardly, barely, very, enough, just, too, completely*.

● *Almost* and *just* are very flexible. They can be used in front of adjectives, and main verbs:

almost full, just visible
He has almost finished. He has just arrived.

● *Just* can also be used in front of nouns when it has a meaning similar to *only*:

These are just weeds, but they are very pretty.
He ate just the meat.

● *Enough* is used after adjectives. It can be used either on its own or in the pattern adjective + *enough* + *to* + infinitive:

Make sure your knife is sharp enough.
Make sure your knife is sharp enough to cut the wood without bending it.

C Language practice ⌖

1 Here are some items you need for a particular hobby or pastime. Guess the two hobbies, and mark the nouns C for countable or U for uncountable.

   a) hammer, wood, nails, drill, saw, glue, varnish

   b) needle, cloth, thread, scissors, pattern, thimble, iron

2 Complete the gaps using *a, the* or – (no article).

> ***a)*** .... *Pasta with* **b)** .... *Lemon Sauce*
>
> | |
> |---|
> | 2 large lemons |
> | 60 g unsalted butter |
> | 85–110 ml cream |
> | white pepper |
> | 455 g fresh pasta |
>
> Peel off **c)** .... zest[1] of one lemon, and put it in **d)** .... frying pan with **e)** .... butter. Cook gently for 5–10 minutes without letting **f)** .... butter burn. Remove **g)** .... zest. Add **h)** .... cream, grate in **i)** .... zest of **j)** .... second lemon, and cook until you have **k)** .... well-flavoured cream.

3 Here are some instructions about how to put up a fence post. Put them into the correct order, using the articles and illustrations to help you.

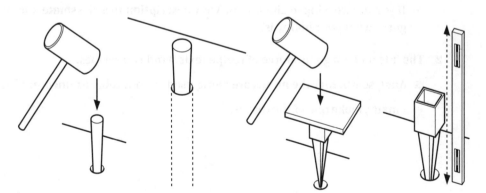

   a) Keep the hole strictly vertical.

   b) Insert a base spike, using a piece of wood on top to prevent damage to the spike.

   c) Make a hole using a steel bar and a heavy hammer.

   d) Check the spike regularly to ensure that it is vertical.

---

[1] *Zest* is the top layer of peel in citrus fruit. It contains oil with a strong scent.

4 **Where would you put the following words in these extracts?**

a) enough

To grow herbs in containers make sure the pot is large to give all the requirements they need when fully grown.

b) almost

Heat the milk until it boils.

c) just

Saw through the plank to half-way.

d) hardly

Sketch the outline first, so that it can be seen, in case you make a mistake.

e) nearly

Whisk in all the cream.

f) barely

Bring the two sheets of metal together until they are touching.

D Follow-up tasks

1 **Think about your favourite hobby or pastime. Think about the preparation needed and the equipment you need for it.**

- Imagine you are explaining your hobby to a beginner. Write some instructions for them.

- If you are working in class, show your description to a classmate. Can they guess what your hobby is?

2 **The internet is a good source of recipe texts. Find two recipes.**

- Analyse whether the nouns are being used as countable or uncountable.

- Finally, make one of the dishes!

UNIT 7 Informal letters and e-mails

Using articles to show shared knowledge

Handling vague language

A Introduction

1 **Which do you prefer writing? Letters or e-mails? Why?**

2 **Look at these extracts from letters and e-mails.**

● **Find the examples which are about similar topics.** ☞

a)
> Thank you for the lunch and useful discussion. I hope we can meet again soon.

b)
> A's back from the exchange visit.

c)
> I must apologise for the problems with the projection equipment.

d)
> Our daughter, Sally, passed her driving test after three
> previous attempts. I have given her my previous car, a
> Citroën. I have bought myself a sports car.

e)
> The food was fab! Let's do it again!

f)
> Sorry about all the stuff yesterday.

g)
> Our son, Alan, is back from a University exchange visit to Philadelphia.

h)
> Sal passed her test (finally!). I've donated the old Citroën to her –
> and bought myself my dream car after all these years!

Think about why ☞

You could probably guess which examples were written in letters and e-mails between friends. How do you know that?

41

Language working in context 🔑

1 Using articles to show shared knowledge

a) Here are some extracts from personal e-mails. Match the topics to the
e-mails: a wedding, a new home, a meal, a football match.

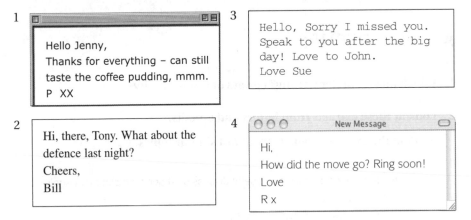

1
> Hello Jenny,
> Thanks for everything – can still
> taste the coffee pudding, mmm.
> P XX

3
> Hello, Sorry I missed you.
> Speak to you after the big
> day! Love to John.
> Love Sue

2
> Hi, there, Tony. What about the
> defence last night?
> Cheers,
> Bill

4 New Message
> Hi,
> How did the move go? Ring soon!
> Love
> R x

b) Why is the definite article used in the above e-mails?

c) Read these extracts about English breakfasts. Underline the nouns. Circle the
nouns which are preceded by articles.

1 Breakfast is different in England. People eat cereal, fried or grilled meat
(such as bacon or sausages) and eggs.

2 On Sunday, the breakfast was really horrible. The eggs were cold and the
coffee was too weak.

3 Breakfasts were generally fine, but nothing like home!

d) Why are articles used differently in the three extracts?

Summary

The choice between no article, *a/an* and *the* often depends on the level of shared
knowledge between writer and reader.

- With an uncountable noun, the choice is between no article (also known as
zero article) and *the*:

Did you get the information? (We both know about this information already.)
Computers process information. (Zero article for a general statement.)

- When using countable nouns, the choice is between *a/an*, *the* and making the
noun plural:

Cars are a major cause of pollution.
Was that the car? (We both know which car, or we have spoken about it before.)
Was that a car? (Perhaps you have just heard a noise.)

2 Handling vague language

a) Here are some lists of items you would have with you in certain circumstances. Match these collective nouns to the lists: *belongings, stuff, tools, kit, things.*

1   going to the gym: change of clothes, trainers, shampoo, towel

2   travelling on an eleven-hour flight: neck pillow, eye-mask, toothpaste, aspirin

3   mending a car: spanner, jack, manual

b) Which of the collective nouns could be used to refer to all the lists of items? Use them to complete this extract from an e-mail.

So I decided to take a taxi because I was feeling so ill, and I got there, paid the driver, stood there wondering what was missing, and then realised I'd left all my .... in the taxi!

Summary

Casual writing between people who know one another often contains vague nouns, or very general collective nouns.

● *Stuff* is used to replace uncountable or plural nouns. It is treated as grammatically singular, even if there are several items:

The suitcases and camera <u>are</u> in the back of the car.
➤ *The stuff <u>is</u> in the back of the car.*

● *Things* is also used as a vague noun, generally when there is a plural noun in mind:
I spent the morning buying things for the new house.

● Other, more formal, options include: *belongings, possessions* and, for specific tasks, *equipment* or *tools.*

● There are also pairs of words which you can use for vague reference: *bits and pieces, bits and bobs, odds and ends, odds and sods* (this last one is very colloquial). These are all used for collections of small items, or when the writer wants to make the items seem slightly unimportant:

I bought some bits and pieces in the sale.

c) **Which of the following extracts from e-mails are accompanied by an attachment. Put 📎 next to them.**

1 Here are some photos from the party!

2 Is there a vegetarian menu?

3 Here's the menu.

4 Let's go this weekend!

d) **Match these replies to the e-mails from the previous activity. What do the underlined words refer to?**

i) ....1... <u>These</u> are awful?! I look terrible!   these = <u>the photos</u>

ii) .... <u>This</u> looks great!   this = ...

iii) .... I'll ask about <u>that</u>.   that = ...

iv) .... <u>That</u>'s a fantastic idea.   that = ...

Think about why ⚭▭

Why can you use *here* in an e-mail or informal letter? Why can you use words like *this* and *that* to refer to things in e-mails?

Summary

● The words *this*, *that*, *these* and *those* are often used to replace a whole noun phrase including any article. You can refer back to things without having to explain them in full. The words are also often used to refer to any attachment, or the contents of the attachment.

The use of *this* and *that* to refer to documents or attachments is similar to the way we refer to things by pointing. We use *this* for things that are very close to us or recent, and *that* for things further away or in the past. If a new document is attached to an e-mail and you are referring to it for the first time you will probably need *this* (or *these*).

Thanks for this!

If you are referring to documents or information you have already talked about you will probably use *that* (or *those*).

I forwarded that on to Simon.

However, people vary in how they use these terms to refer to things. This is because it depends partly on how new we consider the information to be.

● Attachments are often introduced by *here*. You might also use this in an informal letter:

Here are the directions to my house.

In a formal letter, the same information would be given using *the enclosed*:

Please find enclosed details of how to find the office.

C Language practice ⟜

1 **Choose the article which is appropriate to the context.**

   a) I sent him <u>a/the</u> letter. (The writer has been planning to send a letter.)

   b) She gave me <u>a/the</u> photograph of herself for my birthday! (The writer is surprised and telling another friend it's a strange present.)

   c) We really need <u>a/the</u> car. (These people have never had a car before.)

   d) They're thinking about selling <u>a/the</u> car. (These people have one car only.)

   e) <u>(zero article)/The flowers</u> are lovely, thank you! (The writer is pleased with the gift.)

   f) <u>A/The</u> man I told you about rang me yesterday. (The writer is reminding the reader about someone.)

   g) <u>A/The</u> man rang, but he didn't leave his name. (The writer is passing on a message.)

   h) I think <u>(zero article)/the flowers</u> are a nice way to say thank you. (The writer is expressing their general opinion.)

2

a) Match the sentence to the context.

   1 the things I put in the bathroom cupboard

   2 the stuff you lent me

   3 the thing he posted last week

   4 lots of stuff I'd already got

   5 the things she said about me

   a) She has left some possessions behind after a visit to a friend.

   b) She doesn't like her birthday presents.

   c) She is angry about some remarks.

   d) She has borrowed some recipe books.

   e) She is waiting to receive a parcel.

b) Replace the underlined words in the sentences. Choose from: *stuff, thing, things, bits and pieces, belongings, equipment.* **(More than one answer is possible.)**

   1 Did John remember to take his <u>briefcase, coat and umbrella</u> when he left?

   2 We've finished the <u>small tasks</u> on the new house.

   3 I forwarded the <u>e-mail attachment</u> you sent me about computer viruses to Andy.

   4 Thanks for the <u>parcel of clothes</u> for the charity sale.

   5 Will the surveyors need to store any <u>tools, measuring devices or containers</u>?

3 **Rewrite the replies using *this*, *that* or *these* to replace a noun phrase.**

   a) (First e-mail:) Are you happy with the arrangement made last week?

   (Reply:) Yes, the arrangement is fine.

   <u>Yes, this is fine. / Yes that's fine.</u>

   b) (First e-mail:) Here are the specifications for the new building.

   (Reply:) The specifications are different from the original document.

   ....

   c) (First e-mail:) The report is attached.

   (Reply:) The information in the report is excellent news!

   ....

4 **Look at the following situations. Write short e-mail replies.**

   a) A close friend has sent you a photo from a party you were both at last week. Thank her and make a comment.

   b) A colleague you work with every day has sent you details of some useful websites to do with your job. Thank her and send her some information she needs.

   c) Your boss has sent you some figures you need for a report. Thank him, and say they are very useful.

   d) Someone says that they have attached a document. Tell them that you can't find it! Ask them to send it again.

D Follow-up tasks

1 **Ask an English-speaking friend a factual question in an e-mail (for example: the date of a sporting event, a classmate's birthday, or when some homework is due in).**

   ● **When they reply, send them another e-mail to say thank you!**

2 **Collect as many letters or e-mails from friends and family as you can (in any language).**

   ● **If the letters are in English, do they contain any of the features you have worked on in this unit? If they are in another language, is there similar use of vague language?**

UNIT 8 Catalogues

A Introduction

1   Do you often receive catalogues in the post? Have you ever ordered something to be delivered from a catalogue, or from the internet?

2   Match the descriptions to the items below. ⌐═

a)   b)   c)   d)

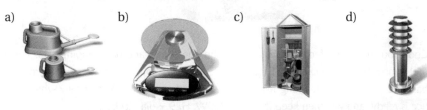

i)

◀ Ideal for use in a variety of locations in your garden, this stainless steel lantern will bring a welcome glow to your garden, driveway or path.

ii)

▲ Style meets convenience in this plastic can for easy watering. Available in three colours and two sizes. The two-litre can is ideal for house plants, while the five-litre can is perfect for outdoors and conservatories.

iii)

▶ Contemporary design with angled display for easy reading and hygienic toughened glass platform resistant to stains. Can be used with or without bowl.

iv)

▼ These easily installed units for garage or garden are made to the highest standards with lockable rubber sealed doors and rubber feet.

Think about why ⌐═

Catalogues are written to sell products and they need to describe the items in very limited space. What effect will these points have on the language used?

1 Building noun phrases using *for* and *with*

a) **Read these descriptions of items from an online catalogue. Complete the gaps using *for* or *with*.**

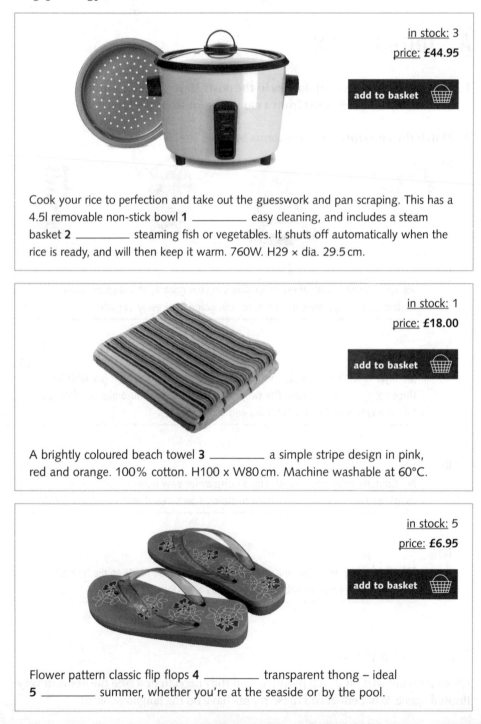

in stock: 3
price: **£44.95**

add to basket 🧺

Cook your rice to perfection and take out the guesswork and pan scraping. This has a 4.5l removable non-stick bowl **1** _____ easy cleaning, and includes a steam basket **2** _____ steaming fish or vegetables. It shuts off automatically when the rice is ready, and will then keep it warm. 760W. H29 × dia. 29.5 cm.

in stock: 1
price: **£18.00**

add to basket 🧺

A brightly coloured beach towel **3** _____ a simple stripe design in pink, red and orange. 100% cotton. H100 x W80 cm. Machine washable at 60°C.

in stock: 5
price: **£6.95**

add to basket 🧺

Flower pattern classic flip flops **4** _____ transparent thong – ideal **5** _____ summer, whether you're at the seaside or by the pool.

b) **Match the items with the correct prepositional phrase.**

1 A pair of glasses
2 The garden bench has a metal coating
3 A USB flash drive
4 A multi-feature printer
5 A tough but light silver metal suitcase
6 A solar powered mobile phone
7 A beautiful gift-boxed set of soaps
8 A jade paper knife

a) for easy cleaning.
b) with high-speed fax facility.
c) with a secure lock and retractable handle.
d) with Polaroid lenses.
e) for saving all your electronic files.
f) with a divine fragrance of roses.
g) for opening your letters in style.
h) for arranging a hot date.

c) **Which preposition links the main noun to other features of the same item?**
Which preposition links the noun to other items or activities?

Think about why 🔑

In the first example of the previous activity the writer could have written *a pair of glasses which have Polaroid lenses*. Why did the writer choose to use *with Polaroid lenses* instead?

Summary

A common way of adding information after a noun is by using *with* or *for*.

- Phrases using *with* show the relationship between the main noun and its features:

  A kitchen clock with large numbers. (The numbers are features of the clock.)

- Phrases using *for* link the main noun to other actions, people and things:

  A kitchen clock for the partially sighted. (The prepositional phrase links the clock to the people who will use it.)

2 Adjectives which take prepositions

a) Put these into the correct order. Add the preposition *for* or *with*.

1 A/two/meal/perfect
   → A perfect meal for two.
   ....

2 folding table/convenient/entertaining outside/This/is/very
   ....

3 are/excellent/coffee/chocolates/These
   ....

4 most types of phone/suitable/that is/mobile phone charger/A
   ....

5 cutting/This/is/a/tool/metal/handy
   ....

6 perfect/This/black scarf/will be/any coat
   ....

7 is/watch/A/a second hand/an/ideal/a sportsman/present
   ....

b) Both prepositions can be used after *perfect*. Is the meaning the same?

Summary

With and *for* are also common after particular adjectives.

● *With* shows that the two things go together well:

  The trousers are perfect with a silk blouse.

● *For* shows that the main noun can be used to complete a task or in a particular situation:

  The shoes are suitable for driving.
  This teddy bear is ideal for a baby gift.

● The following adjectives can take either *with* or *for*:

  excellent, ideal, just the thing, perfect, useful

1 **Shorten these sentences by creating noun phrases with *for* or *with*.**

a) A patterned towel which has a fish design on the borders.

→ A patterned towel with a fish design on the borders.

b)  A wide-brimmed yellow hat which keeps the sun off your face.

....

....

c) A white sarong which has pink flowers on it.

....

d)  A parasol which has a red stripe pattern.

....

....

e) A lovely yellow beach bag you can carry your swimming things in.

....

....

f) A natural citrus spray that will prevent insect bites.

....

2 **Complete the descriptions with a suitable adjective and *for* or *with*. Use a different adjective in each example.**

a) A set of pearl and crystal earrings, ... the matching brooch shown on page 15.

b) A pair of elegant sunglasses with full UV sun protection, ...
lazing on the beach, but making that fashion statement.

c) An inflatable neck pillow with an embroidered pouch, ...
long distance flights.

d) A gift set of aromatic coffees from around the globe, ... our after dinner chocolates.

e) A yellow, plastic lamp in the shape of a cat, ... a child's bedroom.

3

a) Match the descriptions to the drawings.

1   2   3   4

a) Fine china mugs showing yachts with multi-coloured sails.

b) Four concave shaped fine china mugs with a feather design.

c) Set of six brightly patterned mugs with a plant and herb design and inner floral detail.

d) Set of four elegant fine china mugs with classic pattern in black and silver.

b) Design two mugs of your own and draw them. Then write a phrase describing each one.

D Follow-up tasks

1   Imagine you are writing descriptions for an online department store.

   ● Make a list of bestsellers for a department you are interested in. Make some notes about the good features of the products or why the customer might use them. Write descriptions for three of the items.

2   Collect as many descriptions of items from catalogues as you can.

   ● See if you can find examples of *with* or *for*. Are they used with adjectives or do they come straight after nouns?

UNIT 9

Technical manuals

Nouns pre-modified by other nouns

Prepositions used to express precise actions

(A) Introduction

1   **What is the most technical subject you studied at school? Did you need to learn a lot of new vocabulary? Why?**

2   **Look at these extracts from instruction manuals.**

   ● **One of the extracts is written for a general reader, the other is for an expert user or technician. Can you identify which?** ⤝

a)

Before you connect to the telephone line you will need to install batteries in your F23500. The batteries are needed to allow the clock, display and handsfree features to work correctly.

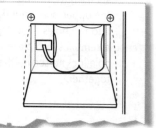

b)

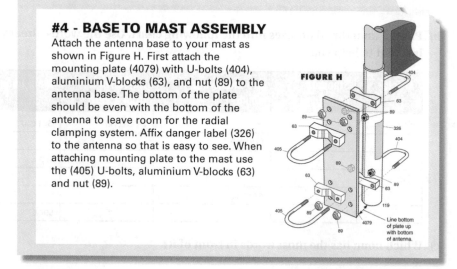

#4 - BASE TO MAST ASSEMBLY

Attach the antenna base to your mast as shown in Figure H. First attach the mounting plate (4079) with U-bolts (404), aluminium V-blocks (63), and nut (89) to the antenna base. The bottom of the plate should be even with the bottom of the antenna to leave room for the radial clamping system. Affix danger label (326) to the antenna so that is easy to see. When attaching mounting plate to the mast use the (405) U-bolts, aluminium V-blocks (63) and nut (89).

FIGURE H

Think about why ⤝

Why is the language of the second extract more difficult than the first? What makes the language difficult?

1 Nouns pre-modified by other nouns

a) **Read these instructions on how to assemble a metal detector. Use your dictionary to find the meaning of the nouns which have been circled. How many meanings does each noun have? Which meaning fits this extract?**

ASSEMBLING YOUR DETECTOR

1 Remove <u>the holding ⟨screw⟩</u> and <u>thumb ⟨nut⟩</u> from <u>the black nylon ⟨pole⟩ tip</u>.

2 Insert the pole tip between <u>the ⟨ears⟩</u> of the searchcoil.

3 On the middle of the pole, press <u>the two spring ⟨buttons⟩</u> and slide the middle pole into the upper pole until the spring buttons click into the holes – locking the two assemblies into place. Tighten <u>the pole ⟨lock⟩</u> to secure the two parts together.

b) **Put the underlined phrases into the following chart. Use the words already inserted to help you.**

Article	Standard adjective	Pre-modifying noun(s)	Adjective from a verb	Main noun
the	–	–	holding	screw
		thumb		
				tip
the				
		spring		
				lock

c) **Which noun has the most words in front of it?**

Think about why 🔑

Words in front of nouns can be either factual (e.g. *square*), or evaluative (e.g. *lovely*), or something in-between (e.g. *big*). Which kind would you expect in technical writing?

Summary

Technical manuals have high frequencies of noun phrases with more than one word in front of a noun. The words that come in front of the main noun are called pre-modifying words:

the red plastic switch (*red and plastic* = pre-modifying words, *switch* = main noun)

A great deal of information can be put in front of a noun. The words used can be other nouns, adjectives, or words formed from verbs:

metal box (noun + noun)
brown table (adjective + noun)
revolving door (adjective from verb + noun)

d) **Circle the nouns which give the material of the second nouns. Not all the examples contain materials.**

1	(fibreglass) insulator	8	plastic bracket
2	horizontal bracket	9	nylon tip
3	pole tip	10	corner screw
4	cable clamp	11	brass nut
5	steel screw	12	handle insulator
6	ring nut	13	alloy bolt
7	assembly bolt	14	metal clamp

e) **Make three-word phrases using the words in brackets.**

1 insulator (fibreglass, handle)
   fibreglass handle insulator

2 connector (corner, plastic)

3 spring (retaining, steel)

4 valve (double, solenoid)

5 window (LED, display)

f) **Now add an adjective of physical description, such as *circular*, *upper* or *black*. Where do you need to put this in relation to the other words?**

Summary

Although they are not fixed, there are patterns to the order of pre-modifying words.

- General uncountable nouns, such as the material the main noun is made from, tend to come before nouns which give local information specific to the technical context:

  steel corner bracket (*steel* (general), *corner* (local/specific))
  rubber linking cable (*rubber* (general), *linking* (local/specific))

- Adjectives come before all the nouns in the phrase, and they also follow a typical order, i.e. size/weight + shape + colour + material + local/specific information + noun(s):

  small, round, black, plastic outer tube

2 Prepositions used to express precise actions

a) **Look at the following instructions. Which examples are from a technical manual and which from a general household manual?**

1 Remove the protective cover carefully.

2 Unscrew the nut until it is 0.25mm above the surface.

3 Position the bolt accurately.

4 Position the bolt under the central hole.

5 Move the switch to position 3, as shown in Figure 5.

6 Unscrew the nut almost completely.

b) **The above instructions follow two patterns: verb + object + adverb or verb + object + prepositional phrase. Mark them A or PP.**

Summary

- The most common sentence pattern in instruction manuals is the following imperative structure: verb + object + prepositional phrase:

  Insert (verb) *the mounting screw* (object) *through the holes* (prepositional phrase).

- Technical instructions use a wide variety of prepositions to express precise physical actions. These form a prepositional phrase after the direct object and function as adverbs:

  Thread the spring <u>into the cylinder</u>.

- Single word adverbs, e.g. *inwards, outwards, securely, carefully* are less precise and less common in technical contexts.

C Language practice

1 **Change these noun phrases so that they are more appropriate for technical writing.**

a) This tube is made of plastic and it's 20 cm.

   → *a 20 cm plastic tube*

b) This is an insulator, it's circular and it's made of fibreglass.

c) This is a hinge on the cover. It's on the front.

d) This is a cable, it's red and it's made of plastic.

e) This is a lock. It's for fixing two parts together. This is for the lower one.

2

a) **Read the instructions for the car seat and label the illustrations 1–6.**

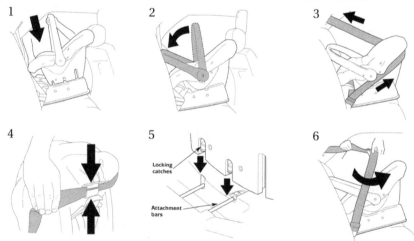

Position the car seat onto the Surefix base (...1...) so that the locking catches on the car seat fit over the attachment bars of the base (......). Push firmly down until the catches on the seat engage. Rotate the handle of the car seat forwards into the 'Fitting' position, see page 3 for more information (......). Wrap the diagonal portion of the vehicle seat belt webbing around the back of the car seat (......). Thread the diagonal section of the vehicle safety belt through the webbing slot in the rear of the car seat backrest (......). Pull the diagonal section of the vehicle seat belt in the direction shown in figure (......) to remove all of the slack so that the car seat is held firmly against the vehicle seat.

b) Look back at the previous text and underline the examples of pre-modified nouns and circle the examples of prepositional phrases.

3 Draw simple diagrams to show the meaning of the prepositional phrases.

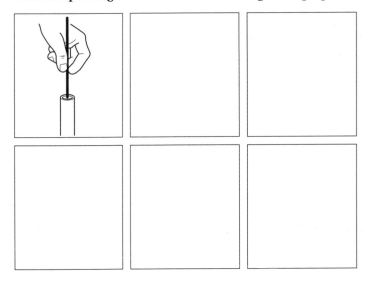

a) into the top of the tube

b) over the tube

c) through the tube

d) between the two tubes

e) around the right-hand tube

f) along the outside of the tube

D Follow-up tasks

1 Find as many examples of technical English as you can. The internet is a good source.

- Do the texts contain examples of the prepositional phrases used in this unit? Do they use any different ones?

2 Find a technical manual in English or one in your own language.

- Analyse some of the noun phrases: how are the main components described? If the manual is in English, are the nouns pre-modified by several other nouns? Do they follow the patterns described in this unit?

- If the manual is in your own language, find some of the nouns used to describe the main parts of the item. Translate them into English using the patterns in this unit.

PART 3

Adding more information to the sentence

(A) Introduction

1 **Do you own an encyclopaedia? Is it a traditional book or is it on a CD-Rom? When do you use it?**

2 **Look at this entry from an encyclopaedia.**

- **Find and underline the words *which* and *whose*. Which words do they relate to?** ⊙➤

Janáček
Eastfoto

Leoš Janáček (1854—1928) Czech composer whose works, such as the operas Jenufa (1904) and Katya Kabanová (1921), are largely based on Czech folk themes.

Janáček was a choirboy at Brno and studied at the Prague, Leipzig, and Vienna conservatories. In 1881 he founded a college of organists at Brno, which he directed until 1920.

He achieved international success as a composer late in life with the performance of his opera Jenufa in Vienna in 1918.

Think about why ⊙➤

What is the main function of an encyclopaedia entry? How does this affect the language used?

B Language working in context ⌐

1 Defining and non-defining relative clauses

a) Underline the relative clauses in this encyclopaedia entry. Put a circle around the noun phrase they are linked to.

> **brick:** ceramic structural material which is made by pressing clay into blocks and firing them in a kiln. Bricks, which in their most primitive form were not fired but were hardened by being dried in the sun, have been used for thousands of years. Examples from approximately 5,000 years ago have been discovered in the Tigris-Euphrates basin, and the ancient races who occupied this region may have been the first users of brick. In Babylonia, where there was a lack of both timber and stone, the thick clay deposited by the overflowing rivers was the only material adaptable to building.

b) Two of the clauses give definitions of the noun phrase and the other two give additional information. Which are they? What do you notice about the punctuation of the different types of relative clause?

Think about why ⌐

Why are relative clauses useful to a writer? Why do writers of informative texts use them?

Summary

- Relative clauses either give necessary information about a noun (define it) or simply add optional information:

  Children who have no brothers and sisters are sometimes shy. (defining relative clause)
  Children, who are treated differently from adults in law, are not responsible for their actions. (non-defining relative clause, adding optional information)

- Non-defining clauses are separated from their noun and from the main verb by a comma. These commas function like brackets[1] and show that the information can be left out without affecting the grammar.

  Using a non-defining relative clause indicates that the writer thinks the material is less important. Choosing whether to use a defining or a non-defining relative clause is, therefore, a matter of focus, as well as grammar.

- *That* is commonly used in place of *which* in defining relative clauses, particularly in US English.

---

[1] *brackets* = ( )

2 Starting a relative clause with a preposition

a) **Match these openings to their relative clauses.**

   1 Steel: alloy of iron and carbon …

   2 Many cognitive psychologists support the 'computer metaphor' …

   3 The various methods …

   4 Ashram: An Indian religious community whose members lead lives of austere self-discipline and dedicated service, …

   a) … by which tallow and other animal fats are separated and purified are dealt with in the article 'Oils, fats and waxes'.

   b) … in which the carbon content ranges up to 2 percent (with a higher carbon content, the material is defined as cast iron).

   c) … in accordance with which the well-known figure Mahatma Gandhi lived his life.

   d) … in which the brain and the computer are seen as having the same characteristics.

b) **What do you notice about the first word(s) of the relative clause?**

Summary

Defining and non-defining relative clauses can start with a preposition. This is needed if the noun would have a preposition in a simple sentence:

She belonged <u>to</u> a society for 40 years. The society awarded her a medal for her achievements as a composer.
➤ *The society, <u>to which</u> she belonged for 40 years, awarded her a medal.*

You grow up <u>in</u> a culture. The culture influences your attitudes.
➤ *The culture <u>in which</u> you grow up influences your attitudes.*

The prepositional element may consist of more than one word:

The system is being designed <u>in accordance with</u> regulations. The regulations are available online.
➤ *The regulations <u>in accordance with which</u> the system is being designed are available online.*

C Language practice 🗝

1 Make each pair of sentences into one sentence by using a relative clause.

a) **impressionism**

A school of painting.
It began in the mid-19th century in France.

A school of painting which began in the mid-19th century in France

b) **aeroplane**

Fixed-wing aircraft is heavier than air.
Fixed-wing aircraft is supported by the dynamic reaction of the air against its wings.

....

c) **Holbein, Hans** (1497–1543)

A painter, born in Augsburg, Germany, the son of Hans Holbein.
His father was also a painter of merit.

....

d) **insects**

Members of the *phylum Arthropoda* have six legs.
The bodies of the members of the *phylum Arthropoda* are divided into three parts.

....

2 Here are some extracts from real encyclopaedias. The relative clauses starting with prepositions have got mixed up. Find them, and put them into the correct definition.

a) **BORON**

A hard, non-metallic solid, which as a pure element does not occur free in nature. It forms many compounds by which good and evil deeds result in appropriate reward or punishment in this life or in a series of rebirths.

b) **BUDDHISM**

A central belief is the law of karma, in which bark formation is prevented; typically caused by bacteria or fungi.

c) **CANKER**

(botany) A general term for a disease of plants, through which it is possible to communicate using long and short sounds in particular patterns which represent letters.

d) **MORSE CODE**

System in which it is bound to oxygen.

3   Each of these encyclopaedia entries is a single sentence. Put them back in order and complete the gaps with the correct preposition. Use the following prepositions: *in, through.*

a) **automated teller machine (ATM)**
    i)   now common outside most banks and building societies
    ii) (......) which money can be withdrawn and other transactions carried out
    iii) the formal name for the 'service tills'

b) **cornett**
    i)   for performing older music
    ii) the cornett has been revived in modern times
    iii) including Bach's cantatas
    iv) (......) which it often doubles the highest voice part

c) **pitcher plant**
    i)   (......) which the leaves are modified to form lidded pitcher traps
    ii) any of the members of three separate families of carnivorous plants
    iii) containing water and enzymes

4 Here are some facts from an online encyclopaedia about helicopters. Write one or two sentences defining helicopters in the style of an encyclopaedia entry. Keep the facts in the same order.

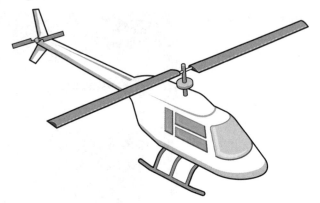

Key points to include:

- Helicopters are a type of aircraft.
- Lift from the ground is obtained in helicopters by horizontal propellers called rotors.
- When the rotor of a helicopter turns it causes a reaction in the body of the helicopter.
- The reaction in the body of the helicopter makes the helicopter spin.
- To compensate for this, many helicopters have a second rotor.
- The second rotor is usually positioned near the tail of the aircraft.

D Follow-up tasks

1 Either using an encyclopaedia or your own general knowledge, write four facts about a famous person.

- Write a sentence about the person. How much information can you include in the one sentence?

- If you are working in class, give your list to another student, but hide the name. Can they guess who it is?

2 Find three articles on the same topic in different encyclopaedias.

- Compare the language in the different sources. Can you find examples of defining and non-defining relative clauses? How many of them start with prepositions?

UNIT 11 Blurbs

Adding information at the start of a clause

Variations in noun pre-modification

A Introduction

1   Have you bought a book or a film recently? Did you read the back of it before you bought it?

2   Look at this blurb[1].

- Can you guess what type of book it is? ⌒➤

Wounded in the line of duty, NYPD detective John Corey is recovering on Long Island when Tom and Judy Gordon are found murdered. Corey knew the young, attractive couple, and Sylvester Maxwell, the local police chief, wants his big-city expertise. Maxwell, however, gets more than he expected.

7801400 99898

- What happened to John Corey before this story begins? Which part of the text gives this information?

Think about why ⌒➤

Apart from giving information, what is the purpose of the blurbs on the back of books and films? What limitation does the writer of these texts have?

[1] A *blurb* is a short text giving information about a book or film.

B Language working in context ⌐

1 Adding information at the start of a clause

a) **Why is the sentence below difficult to read?**

> Ellen May Peters, who was *brought up in an isolated community in the Scottish Highlands where reading any book except the Bible on Sunday was forbidden*, is suddenly thrown into the exciting world of London of the 1880s when her parents die and she is taken to live with her rich aunt.

b) **Can you rewrite this sentence, making it easier to read? Move the sentence in italics and make any grammatical changes necessary.**

Think about why ⌐

The space available on the back of a book or video is very limited. What effect does this have on the language?

Summary

In narratives, relative clauses give background information about something that has already happened.

Passive forms of relative clauses can be placed at the start of sentences. The relative pronoun and any auxiliary verb are not used:

John Brown, who was kidnapped by aliens in 1944, finds life very different when he returns to earth fifty years later.
➤ *Kidnapped by aliens in 1944, John Brown finds life very different when he returns to earth fifty years later.*

Information placed at the start of the sentence in this way is easier to understand than if it comes between the subject and the verb.

Although this form is popular when space is limited, it can also be used in any text to vary the style:

Spoken by millions worldwide, English is also the primary language of the internet.

c) **Match the full sentences to the appropriate relative clauses.**

Billy Bowler had a full life:
1   His work did not interest him and he began committing robberies.
2   The police were almost certain he was guilty.
3   He left the USA and was kidnapped.
4   He returned home, but the authorities thought he was still in Chile.
5   Billy Bowler found love late in life.
6   Sadly, his marriage did not last long and soon he was alone again.

a) *Bored* by his job he took to crime …

b) **Captured** by terrorists …

c) *Believed* by the FBI to be in South America …

d) **Divorced** three years later …

e) *Suspected* by police …

f) **Born** in 1910 and **married** in 1958 …

d) **What is the difference between the words in italics and the words in bold?**

Summary

- Background information can be in the form of actions or states. Past participles introduce actions that have happened to the subject. These are created from passive sentences:

  The Guggenheim museum in Bilbao was designed by Frank Gehry. It is a spectacular building.
  → Designed by Frank Gehry, the Guggenheim museum in Bilbao is a spectacular building.

- Some adjectives can also be used to give background information at the start of a sentence. These adjectives usually describe beliefs other people have about someone (e.g. *suspected, accused, blamed*), or emotional states (e.g. *bored, happy, thrilled, puzzled*). These are created from *be* sentences:

  Samira was excited by the offer. She accepted the job without another thought.
  → Excited by the offer, Samira accepted the job without another thought.

2 Variations in noun pre-modification

a) **Here are three openings to book or film blurbs. Match the extracts to the following topics: a spy thriller, a romantic novel, a detective novel.**

  1 Childhood <u>sweethearts</u>, long ago separated, meet again and innocent <u>love</u> reawakens as desire.

  2 The painting belongs to an unpopular local <u>artist</u>, Campbell, whose body is discovered lying on the rocks below the popular view <u>point</u>.

  3 Some say George Smiley is in innocent <u>retirement</u>. Others say he was sacked after the Czech <u>scandal</u>.

b) **Look at the nouns which have been underlined. Circle the words which define them. What parts of speech are they?**

Summary

The two main forms of pre-modification in these kinds of text are:
one or more adjective(s) + noun, e.g. *innocent love, an unpopular local artist*
one or more noun(s) + noun, e.g. *childhood sweethearts, her father's record collection.*

- Adjectives can be co-ordinated and both adjectives will apply equally to the main noun:

happy and innocent love
a popular but deeply unhappy artist

The same relationship can be shown with a comma:

a beautiful, young woman

- Nouns are not co-ordinated in this way:

~~Enemy and army spies~~ ✗
➤ *Enemy army spies*

C Language practice ⟊

1 **Which part of these extracts could be moved to the start? Write the opening of a new version for each.**

a) Peter Sterling, who was fired by his employers after he was accused of stealing from them, but who is now the head of the largest investment bank in Europe, decides to seek a sinister revenge on his accusers in this fascinating thriller set in the City of London.

....

....

b) Chicago detective Ronny Hale, who was shot while preventing an armed robbery and who is now living in a small village in the south of France, soon realises that he has not left the past behind him.

....

....

c) The Palazzo D'or, which was once owned by a Contessa suspected of having committed three murders, and which was sold to the multi-millionaire businessman Orlando Wei for the highest price ever paid for a building in Europe, reveals its terrible long-held secrets to the young daughter of Mr Wei in this frightening story of love and death.

....

....

....

2 Make each pair of sentences into one sentence starting with a past participle or adjective.

a) Our hero was wounded in the jungle. He managed to walk 50 km to safety.

→ *Wounded in the jungle, our hero managed to walk 50km to safety.*

b) The criminals were thought to be in France. They were really in America.

....

c) Jean-Paul was separated from his parents at the age of 2. He was finally reunited with his family at the age of 35.

....

d) Kita Mara was sold into slavery and never taught to read or write. She eventually escaped, gained an education and wrote her gripping life-story.

....

e) Jane Peterson was suspected of spying. She was found guilty. She spent 10 years trying to prove her innocence.

....

f) Pete Lee was rescued by the gentle people of the planet Zar. He was told by them the secret of eternal youth. He was questioned by the FBI on his return to Earth.

....

3 Here is part of the blurb for the film 'Jurassic Park'. Put the nouns back into the text. Choose the correct noun on the basis of the pre-modifying words.

grandchildren   dinosaurs   predators   inhabitants
entrepreneur   girlfriend   island

On a remote **a)** ...., a wealthy **b)** .... secretly creates a theme park featuring living **c)** .... created from prehistoric DNA. Before opening it to the public, he invites a top palaeontologist and his paleobotanist[1] **d)** .... , a renowned mathematician, and his two eager **e)** .... to experience the park. But their visit is anything but tranquil as the prehistoric **f)** .... break out and begin hunting the island's human **g)** ....

_____

[1] A *palaeontologist* studies dinosaurs, and a *paleobotanist* studies extinct/ancient plants.

4 Put the words in brackets in the correct order in front of the noun.

a) A .... story.
(and/dramatic/deeply moving/love)

b) A .... laboratory.
(secret/research/disease)

c) A .... woman.
(shy/passionate/young/but)

d) A .... drama.
(laugh-a-minute/comedy)

e) A/An .... thriller.
(action/fast-moving)

5 Here is a brief story plot. Create the opening sentences of a blurb that will attract the reader and make them buy the book!

- There are some extremely rare diamonds – known as the rose petal stones.
- The diamonds are stolen.
- They are stolen by Madam Xara – a famous female burglar.
- She hides them in the collar of her pet cat.
- They are finally recovered after a thrilling chase across three continents.

D Follow-up tasks

1 Write a blurb for your favourite film or book.

- **Put some background information about what happens to the central character into a passive relative clause and move this into the start of the opening sentence.**

- **If you are working in class, don't write the title, but show your text to a partner. Can they guess the film or book, or what kind of story it is?**

2 Find a selection of blurbs on books and videos.

- **Can you find any relative clauses at the start of sentences? What patterns of pre-modification to nouns can you find?**

UNIT 12 Holiday brochures

A Introduction

1 **What is your favourite holiday destination? Do you have a favourite hotel there? Describe it and say why you like it.**

2 **Look at these extracts describing three different hotels.**

   ● **Match the star rating to the hotel.** ⊙⟞

   ✱✱✱✱ = luxury, with lots of modern facilities
   ✱✱✱ = quite basic facilities, but in a good location
   ✱✱ = good value and well located, but with not many facilities (no restaurant)
   ---

   a)
   Very well-situated at the beginning of Las Ramblas and near to Catalonia Square, the family-run Vista is full of character. 69 modestly furnished rooms with shower/bathroom, TV, telephone, hairdryer and air conditioning. Lounge, bar, newly opened restaurant la Lluna and lift.

   b)
   Situated in an imposing building in an elegant area of the city the Santa Cruz is a unique hotel. The 124 rooms have a modern yet classical feel, with shower/bathroom, TV, telephone, mini-bar, safe, hairdryer and air conditioning. Lounge, bar, restaurants, sauna and fitness centre.

   c)
   The Casa is a small, simple hotel which enjoys an excellent location in the lively Gothic area. The 38 basic rooms were recently refurbished and have shower, TV, telephone and air conditioning. Other hotel facilities include breakfast room and lift.

Think about why ⊙⟞

How can a writer put a list of things into a sentence? Why are lists common in brochures?

Language working in context ⌐⊸

1 Expanding the sentence using co-ordination

a) **Complete these extracts using the phrases given.**

1 For the discerning .... traveller, the hotel
accommodation is a haven of ....

2 All our rooms have a .... feel, with wireless
internet connection, DVD player and walk-in shower.

3 Start your day with a reasonably priced breakfast in our restaurant

....

a) comfort and tranquillity

b) understated yet luxurious

c) business or leisure

d) and relax in the lounge in the evening

Think about why ⌐⊸

What do you notice about the words on either side of the words *and*, *yet* and *or*?
Why is this?

Summary

● Co-ordinating words include *and*, *but*, *yet* and *or*. They link together units of
the same grammatical function. These work together as one grammatical unit:

A <u>wood</u> and <u>silver</u> bracelet. (noun + noun)
He was <u>cold</u> and <u>hungry</u>. (adjective + adjective)
She couldn't move her arm <u>up</u> or <u>down</u>. (adverb + adverb)

● Writers find co-ordination particularly useful if they want to list several things.
All the items in the list are written with commas separating them, and then the
last item in the list is preceded by the co-ordinating word without a comma:

*The health inspectors indicated they had concerns about storage, preparation,
layout, emergency procedures <u>and</u> the qualifications of the chef. The restaurant
was closed immediately.*

b) The word *and* shows there is co-ordination in a sentence. Underline the parts of the sentence that are being co-ordinated in the following examples.

1 This charming, traditional hotel offers a refined style and comfortable guest rooms.

2 The elegant lobby and impressive guest rooms are ideal for today's traveller.

3 Original marble stairs have been polished and layers of paint removed to reveal beautifully detailed ironwork dating from 1902.

4 Guests receive a complimentary continental breakfast and will enjoy microwaves, refrigerators and coffeemakers in their suites.

c) Circle the verbs in the sentences above. Look at how the parts of the sentence relate to the verb and match them to the following patterns of co-ordination:

i) verb + object + *and* + object

ii) subject + verb + *and* + subject + verb

iii) subject + verb + object + *and* + (subject) + verb + object

iv) subject + *and* + subject + verb

Summary

Sentences and clauses can also be expanded by co-ordination.

● If you are co-ordinating subjects or objects in relation to a single verb, it's quite easy. If there are two or more things of the same kind in your answer, you can combine them:

Saving money and buying a house are things many young people dream of.
(subject + *and* + subject + verb)

They bought a cooker, washing machine and new tumble dryer in the sale.
(verb + object, object + *and* + object)

● If you are co-ordinating two verbs, then the structure of the second clause depends on whether it has the same subject as the first clause:

The hotel was completely modernised in 1999. The hotel has high-speed internet access in all rooms.
➤ *The hotel was completely modernised in 1999, and has high-speed internet access in all rooms.* (You need both verbs as they are different. There's no need to repeat *the hotel*.)

The baths are marble. The taps are gold.
➤ *The baths are marble, and the taps gold.* (You need both subjects because there are two topics. There's no need to repeat the verb.)

You need to use a comma before the co-ordinating word when you are linking clauses.

2 Handling adjective choices

a) **Think of as many antonyms as you can for each of these common adjectives.**

1 elegant ....

2 modern ....

3 classical ....

4 small ....

5 bright ....

6 excellent ....

7 comfortable ....

8 luxurious ....

b) **Which words would you be most likely to find in a brochure?**

c) **Look at the underlined adjectives in this extract and decide whether they are evaluative or factual. Mark them E or F. (Evaluative adjectives depend on the opinion of the writer. Factual adjectives are objective or can be measured.)**

Relax ...

in one of our <u>spacious</u>, <u>new</u> guest rooms,
featuring a <u>comfortable</u> seating area,
<u>large</u> oakwood desk, <u>two</u> phones with
data ports, high-speed internet access,
and in-room coffee.

Summary

Brochure texts contain a high number of positive adjectives. Even when a less positive aspect is described, the adjectives will still focus on the positive, e.g. *simple* rather than *bare*.

- Adjectives in English can be:

  factual, e.g. describing colour or material of a noun
  a red wooden chair.

  evaluative, e.g. giving the author's view
  a lovely, elegant chair

- When evaluative adjectives are combined with factual adjectives, evaluation comes first:
  a fantastic oval swimming pool

C Language practice

1

a) Underline all the co-ordinating words in this extract from an online description of a hotel. What parts of the sentence are co-ordinated? Put brackets around them.

Located right off the prestigious Champs Elysées Avenue, at the crossroads of fashion, entertainment and business, the legendary luxury four-star Sasha Champs Elysées radiates an incomparable charm which has seduced an elegant and international clientele. The hotel's décor is inspired by nature, and the team of staff are dedicated to service. Hotel Sasha offers the chance to experience the very best of Paris life, and gives the business or holiday traveller a feast of traditional services and modern facilities.

b) Find the adjectives and nouns used as adjectives and list them below.

....

....

c) Do you think the words in your lists are factual or evaluative? Mark them F or E.

2 The description of Hotel Sasha goes on to describe the restaurant facilities. Rewrite the following description so that it is more appropriate for a brochure and then compare it with the original text in the key.

Sasha Champs Elysées is a place where the facilities are good. Eat a meal at the hotel restaurant. Visit Sasha's lounge bar: it's very nice.

....

....

3 Put the co-ordinated elements back into this description of a hotel in Rome.

a) and congress

b) and internet connection

c) and an executive floor

d) and Spanish

Melia Verdi

The hotel Melia Verdi has 270 rooms which offer a wide range of comforts: telephone with direct line, satellite TV, air conditioning, mini-bar, modem
a) ...., marble bathroom, outdoor swimming pool, welcome piano bar, fitness trail, courtesy bus timetable, two restaurants with Italian **b)** .... specialities
c) .... The hotel is an ideal location for modern business necessities placing at its guests' disposal: conference rooms, show room, business **d)** .... centre with a 700 seating capacity.

4   Here is a list of facilities you might find in a hotel. Decide which ones you
    want to highlight in a description of a hotel. Write a description using the
    extract in the previous activity as a model.

- [ ] air-conditioned
- [ ] alarm clock
- [ ] babysitting
- [ ] balcony
- [ ] bar
- [ ] barber shop
- [ ] boutiques
- [ ] business centre
- [ ] car rental desk
- [ ] coffee shop
- [ ] currency exchange
- [ ] doctor-on-call

- [ ] drugstore
- [ ] exercise gym
- [ ] florist
- [ ] 24-hour front desk
- [ ] games room
- [ ] hairdryer in room
- [ ] heated pool
- [ ] international direct dial
- [ ] jogging track
- [ ] laundromat
- [ ] lounge
- [ ] mini-bar

- [ ] multilingual
- [ ] newsstand
- [ ] parking
- [ ] poolside snack bar
- [ ] restaurant
- [ ] room service
- [ ] safe deposit box
- [ ] sauna
- [ ] smoke detectors
- [ ] solarium

D   Follow-up tasks

1   Think of your favourite hotel or imagine a hotel where you would like to stay.

   ● Write a basic factual description.

   ● Decide how to make the description more attractive. If you are working in
     class, show it to a classmate and ask them to help you.

2   If you have access to the internet, visit a site offering holidays.

   ● Are there lots of adjectives? Make a list of them, and decide which are
     evaluative and which are factual.

UNIT 13 Travel guides

Adding information to the noun by apposition

Varying the style by moving appositional phrases

(A) Introduction

1 **What is your favourite city? How would you describe it?**

2 **Look at this extract from a travel guide.**

● **Can you guess which city is being described, and fill in the gaps?** ⌐━

> Once the capital of the greatest empire the world has ever known,
> **a)** _____ is still Europe's largest city and is embedded in
> the culture, vocabulary and dreams of **b)** _____ speakers
> worldwide. At times it will be more grand, evocative, beautiful and
> stimulating than you could have imagined; at others it will be colder,
> greyer, dirtier and more expensive than you believed possible.
>
>
>
> **c)** _____'s
> main geographical feature is
> the **d)** _____, a
> tidal river that enabled an
> easily defended port to be
> established far from the
> dangers of the English
> Channel. Flowing around
> wide bends from west to
> east, it divides the city into
> northern and southern
> halves.

Think about why ⌐━

Will the description of the same city be written differently in different contexts, for
example: a travel guide book, a holiday brochure or an encyclopaedia? Why?

B Language working in context ⌐

1 Adding information to the noun by apposition

a) Find the best ending for these sentences.

1   Athens, <u>home of the 2004 Olympics</u>,

2   Singapore, <u>a busy trading centre in the early 19th century</u>,

3   Mountainous St Kitts, <u>the first English settlement in the Leeward Islands</u>,

a)   … is one of the fastest growing Asian economies.

b)   … crams some stunning scenery into its 65 square miles (168 square km).

c)   … has a population of 4 million living in a fascinating mix of ancient and modern.

b) Could you remove the underlined words from the sentences? What do they add to the sentence?

Summary

Basic apposition adds information as a phrase after a noun. It places the information between commas, next to the noun it describes:

Ningbo, a thriving city south of Shanghai, has a population of 5 million.

The sentence remains grammatically complete without the appositional phrase:

Ningbo has a population of 5 million.

c) Complete the sentences using the phrases given.

1   Cardiff, ..., is to the west.

2   The park, ..., is Indonesia's premier wildlife reserve.

3   Tokyo, ..., is in fact a series of small towns and villages.

4   The Louvre, ..., is a stunning mix of old and new.

5   Thailand, ..., has something for everyone.

6   Berlin's Reichstag building, ..., is the home of the Bundestag, ...

a) on the southwestern tip of Java

b) with its new Welsh parliament building and rugby stadium

c) Germany's parliament

d) beautiful, intriguing and very easy to travel around

e) built in 1200 as a fortress

f) redesigned by architect Norman Foster and rebuilt during the 1990s

g) one of the world's largest and most complex cities

d) Why is the phrase *with its new Welsh parliament building and rugby stadium* different from the rest?

Think about why ⌐

Why is apposition so common in guide book writing? And why is it useful to writers, generally?

Summary

A range of phrases can be used appositionally:

● noun phrases

These expand the information by describing the first noun in a new way:

The nearest thing to a centre is Union Square, <u>San Francisco's liveliest urban space</u>, populated in equal degree by high-style shoppers, eager street musicians and out-of-it tramps and beggars.

● prepositional phrases

Nottingham, <u>in the heart of the English Midlands</u>, is a compact city with a number of links to Britain's industrial and literary past.

● '*with its*' phrases

A special kind of prepositional phrase is the '*with its*' phrase. These are a particularly flexible way of introducing a number of facts about the main noun, generally referring back to it:

Bilbao, <u>with its lovely mix of classical and modern architecture, crazy cow sculptures, and a great night life</u>, is less famous than Barcelona, but well worth a visit.

● adjective phrases (including adjectives formed from past participles of verbs)

Singapore, <u>connected by a causeway to Malaysia</u>, measures only 622 sq km, yet it is home to more than 3 million people.

2 Varying the style by moving appositional phrases

a) Underline the appositional phrases.

Stockholm, the country's capital, is remarkably peaceful despite having a population of 1.6 million. Stockholm, with its bars and clubs, is a progressive city, though there are pockets which have a village feel. Gamla Stan, the fascinating old town built in the 13th century, is a good place to begin to explore.

b) Rewrite the text varying the style in the following ways:

1   Move the *with its* phrase before the noun.

2   Rewrite the final sentence so that it begins with *A good place …*

c) Which version of the text do you prefer?

Summary

Different stylistic effects are created depending on where you put the appositional element. Their positioning can make the writing more lively, or change the emphasis.

- Delaying the subject noun has the effect of making the style more vivid and journalistic:

  A home to 12 million people, London also welcomes 26 million visitors a year.

- Placing the apposition after the subject is rather neutral and has the effect of a standard non-defining relative clause:

  London, (which is) a home to 12 million people, also welcomes 26 million visitors a year.

- Positioning the appositional element after an object or complement gives it the most emphasis:

  My favourite city is Barcelona, a city of magical architecture.

1 **Look at these examples from guide books. Where could you add the phrases in italics? Put ▲ where you think the phrase should go.**

a) Edinburgh only became Scotland's capital at the end of the Middle Ages.

… a favoured royal residence from the 11ᵗʰ to 16ᵗʰ centuries …

▲Edinburgh only became Scotland's capital …

Edinburgh ▲ only became Scotland's capital …

b) Dublin is home to many students.

… with its universities and professional schools …

c) The modern capital of Italy is Rome.

… the most ancient and venerable city in the country …

d) London is still an important centre for trade.

… once the home of the busiest ports in the world …

e) Here on Java we find the largest Buddhist Temple in the world.

… the Borobudur Temple built in the year of 825 …

2 **Combine the sentences into a single sentence using the underlined phrases as appositional phrases. Use the prompts to help you.**

a) Although ....

Most of the visitors head for the beaches of Cancun.

Many others visit the area for its many Mayan archaeological sites.

Cancun is <u>a major resort city in the northeastern part of the Yucatan.</u>

b) Recognised ....

Penang Island is recognised as the 'Pearl of the Orient'. <u>It is a fabulous destination</u>. Penang is renowned for its superb beaches and exotic sights.

c) Created ...., the garden...

The garden of Dembo-in was created in the 17th century by Kobori Enshu. Kobori Enshu was <u>the genius of Zen landscape</u>. The garden of Dembo-in is the best-kept secret in Asakusa.

3 **Here are some facts about the island of Madagascar. Combine them into a paragraph which will both inform the reader and keep them interested.**

- an island
- located in the Indian Ocean
- a nature lover's dream
- was cut off from the African mainland for millions of years
- has types of animals and plants preserved that are found nowhere else in the world
- You can see all these in a spectacular collection of accessible national parks.

(D) Follow-up tasks

1 **Find a selection of guide book articles or read some online.**

- **Analyse the appositional phrases you find. Categorise them according to whether they are noun phrases, prepositional/'with its' phrases, or adjective phrases. Try to move them into a different position.**

- **If you are working in class, discuss the effect this has and which version you prefer.**

2 **Write a short paragraph describing your favourite holiday destination.**

- **Use at least two appositional phrases in your text.**

- **If you are working in class, leave out the name of the place and any other clues and see if your partner can guess the location.**

14 Direct mail

Adding comparative and superlative structures to the sentence

Adjectives that do not normally take comparative or superlative forms

A Introduction

1   How often do you receive mail trying to sell you something? Can you guess that it is junk mail[1] from the envelope? Do you put these letters in the rubbish straight away? Or do you read them?

2   Here is an extract from a direct mail letter.

● Find synonyms in the text for the following: *most exciting, less difficult, more pleasant, highest quality.* ⌐━

We know there is nothing nicer than selecting a present for a loved one, and it's easy when you look through our specially selected items. All you have to do is sit back, and at your leisure choose from its plentiful contents. Nothing could be simpler.

Imagine settling down in front of a blazing fire, drinking from our finest champagne flutes. The gifts have been carefully selected to make this your most thrilling Christmas ever.

Making a purchase from this fine selection couldn't be easier.

Think about why ⌐━

Why might letters be a better way of selling things than an advertisement in a magazine?

---

[1] *Junk mail* is mail trying to sell you something.

B Language working in context ⌐

1 Adding comparative and superlative structures to the sentence

a) Look at these extracts from direct mail letters. Match them to the type of organisation they were sent from. Choose from the following: a magazine, a charity, a mobile phone company, a hotel company.

1

> By supporting us and starting a regular gift today, you can help bring about a better future.

2

> **Global News** will add the ideal international angle to your national newspapers and local news magazines – the most important 60 minutes of your week.

3

> For this month only, we're offering a choice of high specification handsets and an even bigger discount.

4

> We are delighted to offer you Europe's most extensive and cheapest range of weekend breaks ever.

b) Find and circle the comparative or superlative adjectives and the nouns they are linked to.

Think about why ⌐

Why do these texts contain so many comparative and superlative forms? Why do some comparisons in adverts end without a second noun, e.g. *an even bigger discount*?

Summary

A very common feature of advertising texts is the use of comparative and superlative adjectives to modify nouns:

> a *cheaper* car than our last one (comparative)
> the *latest* edition (superlative)

- Comparatives and superlatives can be co-ordinated in front of a noun:

> The report was longer than in 2004. It was also more complex.
> ➤ … a longer and more complex report than in 2004 …

- Comparative forms require a second noun so that the reader knows what the first noun is being compared with. These are introduced by *than*. However, in some contexts this second noun is simply understood and can be omitted:

> Can I have more ice, please? (The comparison is understood from the context.)

Leaving out the second noun can be very useful for writers of advertisements. It means you can suggest a positive comparison without specifying exactly what your product is better or cheaper than!

> We'll give you a better package – guaranteed!

c) Match the openings of these sentences to the endings.

1. Nothing could be easier …
2. Placing an order online …
3. There is nothing simpler …
4. It couldn't be easier …

a) … than buying from our latest online selection.
b) … than opening a Highway account.
c) … to change your account to us.
d) … couldn't be simpler.

Summary

Various negative constructions can also be used to express comparative meanings.

- Using *nothing* and a comparison strengthens the meaning and makes it more emphatic.

> A holiday for two in Barbados is romantic.
> ➤ *Nothing* could be more romantic than a dream holiday for two in Barbados.

> A day in the country is relaxing.
> ➤ *There is nothing* more relaxing than a day in the country.

- *Couldn't* is also used in the pattern noun/–*ing* form + *couldn't be* + comparative form:

> Getting a loan from us couldn't be easier.

2 Adjectives that do not normally take comparative or superlative forms

a) **Which of the words in bold would you choose in the following context? And why?**

To say thank you for filling in the survey, we'll enter you into our free prize draw. A fabulous holiday for two is on offer. And even **more perfect/better**, you can choose the destination!

b) **Complete the chart with the comparative and superlative forms.**

adjective	comparative	superlative
good	better	best
perfect	(not possible)	(not possible)
acclaimed		
beautiful		
global		
favourite		
exclusive		
unique		
unrivalled		

Summary

- Some adjectives are rarely, or never, used in comparative or superlative forms. These adjectives express an absolute meaning which does not allow degree:

  unrivalled ➜ ~~more unrivalled~~ / ~~most unrivalled~~ ✗

- Certain technical terms are also not usually found in comparative or superlative forms, e.g. *circular, horizontal*.

C Language practice 🔑

1 Underline the comparative and superlative forms and complete the gaps. Choose from the following nouns: *brochure, competition, discounts, way, writers.*

a)
> We even give you the choice of how you want to apply. The quickest and most popular .... is over the phone.

b)
> *We are the only company to offer free travel insurance and even higher ....*

c)
> It is a pleasure to introduce our latest and, we humbly suggest, most comprehensive worldwide holidays special offer ....

d)
> VF brings together the greatest photographers and .... in an exciting new publication.

e)
> # Bigger, better, brighter.

f)
> *Please help make our Autumn .... our best ever by buying the enclosed tickets or selling them to friends, family and colleagues.*

2 Can you use these adjectives in comparative and superlative forms?

a) red
b) oval
c) popular
d) online
e) one-off

f) spacious
g) far
h) chemical
i) dramatic
j) minimal

3   Look at this advert for diet foods. Add the comparative and superlative forms of the following adjectives: *good, tasty, high (×2), low (×2).*

We've made big changes to our WatchUWay meals –
a) .... fibre, **b)** .... fat, the
c) .... ever cholesterol levels, and an even
d) .... range of vitamins. But we've kept everything you said you liked. And most importantly we can offer you the **e)** .... quality and
f) .... meals ever!

4

a) Choose one item from each column to make sentences which could be used in an advertising letter.

It	is	you more benefits.
There	couldn't be	easier to apply.
Driving to work	gives	nothing more challenging.
No one		more fun.

....

....

....

b) Think of products the sentences might be used to sell.

D   Follow-up tasks

1   Write your own advert.

● The advert is for a new range of women's clothes. The focus of the advert is on the changes that have been made to a famous brand of clothes. The old range was mainly for middle-aged people. The makers want to appeal to younger buyers, but also want to reassure existing customers that the quality is still the same!

● Here are some adjectives to help you: *bright, funky, cute, sexy, elegant, pretty, chic, stylish, attractive, stunning, adorable, eye-catching.*

2   Collect as many direct mail letters as you can, or find a selection of advertisements with text.

● Do they contain examples of comparative and superlative forms? Are there any different examples from the ones you have worked on in this unit? Are there any examples of comparisons without a second noun?

PART 4

Sequencing and focusing

UNIT 15 Everyday instruction booklets

Non-finite clauses: *–ing* and *to* ...

Prepositions introducing *–ing* clauses

A Introduction

1 ● Have you bought any new household equipment recently?

● Make a list of electrical equipment you might need at home. Which kinds of equipment need an instruction booklet?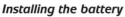

2 Here are the instructions for a new household telephone.

● Underline all the words ending in *–ing*.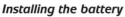

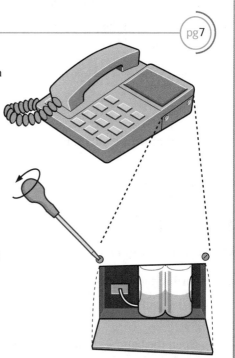

> pg 7

Installing the battery
▶ Open the battery compartment using a small screwdriver to undo the screw. Insert the battery.

Connecting the telephone line
▶ Plug the telephone line cord into the telephone wall socket.

Save button
▶ After dialling the number but before you replace the handset, press the save button. The number dialled is now stored under the save button and can be dialled at another time.

Think about why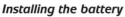

The *–ing* forms above focus on actions. Why are these forms common in instruction booklets?

B Language working in context 🔑

1 Non-finite clauses: –*ing* and *to* …

a) Look at these headings from instruction booklets. Decide whether they are instructions on how to use a cooker, a freezer or could be for either. Mark them C, F or E.

1 Grilling meats

2 Cleaning the interior

3 Storing fresh foods

4 Changing the light bulb

5 Setting the temperature

6 Using the auto-defrost function

7 Adjusting the time

b) Complete these instructions using headings from the previous activity. Change the headings from –*ing* to *to* + *infinitive*.

1 *To set the temperature,* .... turn the dial in a clockwise direction.

2 ...., switch on the grill function.

3 ...., press the buttons marked H and M.

4 ...., ensure the appliance is switched off and remove the old bulb.

5 ...., switch off the appliance and wash with a damp cloth.

Think about why 🔑

Which form, –*ing* or *to* + *infinitive*, is most common as a heading?

c) Underline the –*ing* forms.

1 Place clothes in the washing machine, shaking them out as much as possible.

2 Open the battery compartment, using a small screwdriver to undo the screw.

3 Close the cover, turning it anti-clockwise.

4 Open the door. Shake the clothes out. Put them in the machine.

d) Are the actions in the instructions above meant to happen after one another (sequentially) or at the same time (simultaneously)? Mark them SEQ or SIM.

e) What form of the verb is used to express simultaneous actions?

Summary

There are two main kinds of non-finite clause: *–ing* and *to* + infinitive.

● In instructions, and elsewhere, *to* + infinitive is used to express an aim and the action linked to it. The pattern is *to* + infinitive + object + imperative:

To make an international call (aim), *dial 00* (action).
To enter the competition (aim), *text us your answer* (action).

● Non-finite *–ing* clauses express a complete action. Therefore, they are often used as headings in a list of actions:

Connecting the aerial.
Using your handset. (Personal pronouns make the style more informal.)

A particular use for *–ing* clauses is to express actions which happen together.

Bring the sauce to the boil, stirring continuously.

2 Prepositions introducing *–ing* clauses

a) **Match the instructions to the appliances.**

1 Adjust the level **by** turning the feet, using your fingers or a spanner.

2 To clean the drinks box we recommend that you rinse it several times with hot water **after** letting the water cool down.

3 **Before** using the machine for the first time, clean thoroughly **by** operating two or three times with the maximum volume of fresh water but **without** using ground coffee.

4 Change the temperature **by** turning the thermostat knob to the required setting.

b) **Which of the prepositions in bold refer to the order in which you do things?**

Summary

A number of prepositions relating to time and sequencing can be used in front of non-finite *–ing* clauses.

● *after* and *before*

After removing the cover, …
Before leaving, …

After and *before* can also be followed by a finite clause with a subject. Household instructions often contain both kinds.

After you remove the lid, … (including subject)
After removing the lid, … (without subject)

● The conjunction *when* can also be used in both ways:

When you turn your phone on or off, the start-up picture appears in the display.
When using a portable handsfree kit, you can choose to answer a call by pressing any key.

● A further set of prepositions (*by, despite, instead of, without, not worth*) also introduce *–ing* clauses, and show how actions are carried out or the range/scope of an action:

Despite removing the lid carefully, she covered herself in paint.
Instead of using a screwdriver, he used a knife.

These prepositions cannot be followed by finite clauses:

Despite ~~she removed the lid carefully,~~ … ✗
Instead of ~~he used a screwdriver,~~ … ✗

C Language practice ☞

1 **Choose objects that can follow these verbs.**

   a) Installing …
   b) Connecting …
   c) Adjusting …
   d) Changing …
   e) Assembling …

i) the telephone line	v) the battery
ii) the volume	vi) the strength
iii) the shelves	vii) the brightness
iv) the time	viii) the monitor

2 Complete the gaps in these instructions. Use the following words: *after, before, when, by.*

a) .... dialling the number but before you replace the handset, press the save button.

b) .... replacing batteries do not mix old and new and do not mix makes and types.

c) .... turning the volume control (button 29), the volume can be changed.

d) .... using the coffee maker for the first time, clean thoroughly.

e) .... pulling the mains cable out of the socket, do not pull on the cable, but on the mains plug.

f) .... switching on the appliance, make sure your hands are dry.

3 Correct the following instructions. There are four mistakes.

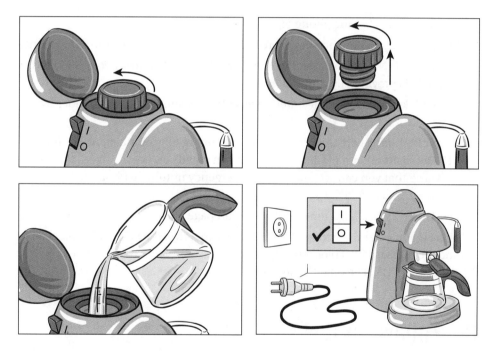

How to make perfect espresso coffee.

a) Open the hinged lid, unscrew the water tank cap by you turn it anti-clockwise.

b) Lift and turn again to remove the cap.

c) To filling the water tank use your glass carafe to measure the volume of water required.

d) Always switching the machine off and remove the plug from the socket before you filling the water tank.

4 Here are some notes about how to use a mobile phone. Complete the text using the correct form of the following verbs: *make, enter, unblock, turn, press*. Some of the verbs are used more than once.

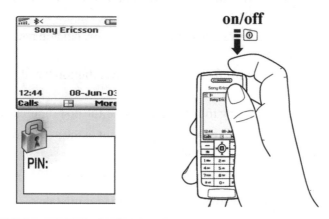

a) .... the phone on.

b) .... on the phone, press the on/off button on the top of the phone.

Enter your PIN (Personal Identity Number), if you have one for your SIM card. Your PIN is provided by your network operator.

If you make a mistake while entering your PIN, delete the wrong number by

c) .... ☐ C .

If your PIN starts with the same digits as an emergency number, for example 112, the digits are not hidden with an * when you **d)** .... them. This is so that you can see and call an emergency number without **e)** .... a PIN.

See '**f)** .... emergency calls' on page 26.

Note: If you enter the wrong PIN three times in a row, the SIM card is blocked and the message 'PIN blocked' appears. **g)** .... it, you need to enter your PUK (Personal Unblocking Key).

Ⓓ Follow-up tasks

1 Write a set of instructions for a household item you have. Include examples of the non-finite clauses you have worked on in this unit.

   ● If you are working in class, see if your partner can understand the instructions and check whether the headings are clear. Ask them to mime the instructions and see if the class can guess what the machine is!

2 Collect as many instruction booklets as you can and analyse the language.

   ● Does the text contain any of the features worked on in this unit? Instruction booklets are often published in many languages. If your language is represented, find out how the non-finite clauses are translated.

16 Newspaper stories

Handling and combining adverbs of time and place

Adverb phrases starting with prepositions

(A) Introduction

1. ● Do you read a daily newspaper? Do you read English language newspapers?

   ● What is the first part of a newspaper that you always read?

2. Look at this newspaper article.

   ● Underline adverbs or adverb phrases which indicate time or location. ⌐━

A SCIENTIST who tried to blackmail[1] food companies by threatening to poison their products was jailed for three years yesterday.

Microbiologist Michael David Brown, 37, had demanded a total of £250,000 from five firms, saying he would poison foods on supermarket shelves with two bacteria if they did not comply.

Brown was arrested in Vienna last month as he tried to withdraw a £50,000 first instalment from a bank in the city.

Yesterday Brown told the court in Vienna that he devised the plan after the failure of a computer firm he ran.

Think about why ⌐━

Newspaper articles giving news stories have to present information clearly and quickly. The main focus is usually on people and an unusual event. What other kinds of information do readers want to know?

---

[1] *Blackmail* is a crime. A blackmailer says that s/he will do something to harm someone, or tell the world a secret about them. The blackmailer asks for money to stop doing this.

B) Language working in context 🔑

1 Handling and combining adverbs of time and place

a) Find the adverbs or adverb phrases of time and location in the following extracts. Mark them T and L.

1 Sparks and ash rained on Sydney yesterday as bushfires[1] jumped a river and roads, and raced towards the suburbs.
   → on Sydney (L), yesterday (T), towards the suburbs (T)

2 A Fokker plane carrying 34 passengers and crew crashed into Manila Bay early today.

   ....

3 Negotiations reopened in Brussels last week. The final round of discussions is due in Amsterdam next June.

   ....

4 European Union leaders are determined to complete a new draft agreement by November ahead of their summit in Dublin in December.

   ....

5 The German Football Association published their report in full on the website.

   ....

b) Complete the following rule using the examples in the previous activity to help you.

When both time and place adverbs are used in a sentence, ...

generally comes before ....

Summary

Newspaper stories are full of facts about when and where events happened. Because space is limited, these are packed into the sentence in the form of adverbs giving time and location.

Adverbs of time and place can be single words (*again, there*), or complete phrases (*last month, in New York*).

Although adverbs are very flexible, there are typical patterns in how adverbs of time and place are used. Location adverbs are often followed by time adverbs.

*Children sang for the President at the airport (*location*) yesterday (*time*).*

---

[1] A bushfire is a fire which sometimes happens in very dry countries and is difficult to stop.

c) Read these two versions of the same story. In the first story all the time and location adverbs and adverbial phrases are in front of the subject. Where are they located in the second story?

1

> Leyton Hewitt must be tempted to think that championship finals are easy. <u>Last year at Flushing Meadows</u> Pete Sampras managed only eight games in a straight-sets defeat against the young Australian, and <u>yesterday</u> David Nalbandian managed only six.

2

> Leyton Hewitt must be tempted to think that championship finals are easy. Pete Sampras managed only eight games in a straight-sets defeat against the young Australian <u>last year at Flushing Meadows</u>, and David Nalbandian managed only six <u>yesterday</u>.

Think about why 🗝

Why do writers move adverbs in front of the subject?

Summary

- There are three main positions in a clause where an adverb can be placed:

  Initial position

  Yesterday the stock market fell by 100 points. (adverb in front of subject)

  Middle position

  The stock market unexpectedly fell by 500 points. (adverb after subject or after first auxiliary verb if there is one)

  End position

  The stock market fell 100 points today. (adverb comes after the verb and object or complement)

- Writers choose the position of adverbs according to focus.

  New topics (e.g. the introduction of a person into the news story for the first time), are not usually introduced with adverb phrases in front of them:

  Share prices rose towards the end of the week. (Introducing topic of share prices.)

  Secondary topics, or topics introduced for contrast, are often preceded by adverb phrases which link them to the main topic or focus of the text:

  By the close of business on Monday the shares had fallen sharply. (Because we already know the topic, the focus can move to time at the start of this sentence.)

  If the writer particularly wants to focus on the time or location for emphasis, the adverbs will open the story.

2 Adverb phrases starting with prepositions

a) **Look at these extracts from newspaper articles. Which of the prepositions in bold could be replaced with *because of*?**

1

YESTERDAY Brown told the court in Vienna that he devised the plan **after** the failure of a computer firm he ran.

2

ALLIED DOMECQ shares rose 5p to 524p **amid** news that new chairman Sir Christopher Hogg wants a demerger[1].

3

AMBULANCE service bosses face legal action from a couple who were injured with their children when an 'unsafe' ambulance overturned as it took them to hospital after a car crash. Several vehicles have been taken off the road and may have to be scrapped **following** the accident at King's Lynn, Norfolk.

Summary

Many adverb phrases introduced by a preposition have special meanings in newspaper texts.

- *amid* (due to / because there were)
  The chairman was fired amid questions about the accounting system.

- *after* (because of)
  The tree was cut down after fears that it was dangerous.

- *ahead of* (prior to / before)
  The President met the Prime Minister ahead of the summit in New York.

- *alongside* (with / at the same time as)
  There were several smaller meetings alongside the main meeting.

- *following* (because of / after)
  The road was redesigned following the accident.

- *in the midst of* (during / because of)
  The editor resigned in the midst of allegations that he had lied.

- *over* (about)
  Fears are growing over the increasing age of the population in Europe.

- *with* (often used to introduce an example or cause)
  Statistics show that economic growth is down, with retailers reporting low sales.

---

[1] A *demerger* is a business term. It means that a large company will be divided into smaller units, and these sold.

C Language practice 🔑

1 **Here are four basic sentences. Add one of the adverbs or adverb phrases to each.**

a) Heavy snow fell.

b) A plane carrying 150 passengers and crew crashed.

c) The kidnappers were arrested.

d) The pound fell sharply against the dollar.

i) just 15 minutes after take-off

ii) in London yesterday

iii) after the release of the victim

iv) amid news of the Prime Minister's resignation

2 **Put adverbs of time and place in the extracts below. Use the adverbs given in italics. Put ▲ where you think the adverbs should go.**

a) The London Stock Market fell sharply again, closing for the first time below the level at which Labour came to power in 1997.

   yesterday

   ....

b) Panic gripped stock markets yesterday after fears of further corporate scandals sent share prices crashing.

   across Europe and America

   ....

c) A survey by the Department of Trade also showed the rate of growth in activity in the service sector fell back.

   last month

   ....

d) There was some lifting of the gloom. The Dow Jones index closed at 9054.97, up 47.2.

   in New York

   ....

e) Predictions that the Bank's Monetary Policy Committee will leave rates at four per cent hardened.

   after figures suggesting the economy's recovery could be in difficulty

   ....

3 Find prepositions in the stories which mean the same as *because*, *with* or *about*.

SCHOOLGIRL QUITS MODELLING CAREER TO TAKE A LEVELS

... But Ella, who has already taken part in fashion shows alongside supermodels Naomi Campbell, Kate Moss and Jodie Kidd, wants to prove she has brains as well as beauty ...

Taxes to rise under Labour

DEBATE continued today over proposals contained in a leaked memo appearing to suggest sharp rises in taxes in the coming budget.

Change at the top

Norway's biggest bank, DN Bank, found a new managing director, Marijke Rule. His predecessor resigned after the bank lost $243m last year from speculating in options.

4 Here is part of an interview with someone who saw a train crash. Use the information from the story to write the beginning of a news story on the same event. Include the main event, the time and the location in the opening sentence.

'It was yesterday morning and I was standing waiting for my bus to go to work, when there was this terrible noise and we all rushed to look over the bridge. The two trains had hit each other. Luckily, one – a goods train – had been stationary and the other one, the one with passengers, had only just started out from Penning Station so it was going really slowly. So no one was hurt very much, just shaken up. I was too!'

....

....

....

D Follow-up tasks

1 Think of a major news event – either one everyone is talking about now, or one from history – and write the opening of a news story about it.

● If you are in class, show it to a classmate. Can they guess what event you are describing?

2 Find three stories in English language newspapers – either paper versions or online. Choose one of the sections of the newspaper you are most interested in. Underline all the time and location adverbs. Do they follow the patterns you have worked on in this unit?

Various styles of instructions

Reduced imperatives

A Introduction

1 Apart from food and drink, what did you buy last time you went to a supermarket? Which of the items would be safe to leave with a child?

2 Look at these directions for a painkiller.

● Underline the different ways of giving instructions which are used. ⚫⌐

Directions:	
The tablets should be swallowed whole with water. Do not chew.	
How much to take:	
Adults and children over 12:	2 tablets to be taken every 4 hours. Do not exceed 8 tablets in 24 hours.
Children 6 – 12 years:	1 capsule every 4 hours. Do not exceed 4 capsules in 24 hours.

Think about why ⚫⌐

Some everyday items you buy do not have directions for use. Why do some of the items need instructions, and others not?

B Language working in context ⌐

1 Various styles of instructions

a) **Mark these items as cosmetics (C), medicines (M), cleaning materials (CM) or foods (F).**

perfume	bleach
powdered milk	facial cleansing cream
washing powder	lipstick
jelly	painkillers
cough mixture	eggs
antiseptic cream	disinfectant

b) **Decide whether these instructions are for cosmetics or for medicines. Mark them C or M.**

1 Adults and children aged 12 years and over: Fill measure cup to 20 ml mark (or four 5 ml spoonfuls). Take just before going to bed.

2 Gently lather onto damp skin morning and evening.

3 Spray onto wet hair, blow dry as normal.

4 Adults aged 18 or over: Two sprays into each nostril every morning and evening. Use regularly.

5 Tilt head, and gently squeeze up to 5 drops into ear.

6 Apply generously. Reapply frequently.

c) **Here are examples of three different styles of instruction. Mark them *active* or *passive*.**

1 You should take the medicine before breakfast.

2 The tablets should be swallowed whole with water.

3 The medicine should be taken before breakfast.

4 Two tablets to be taken every four hours.

5 You should take 2 tablets every 4 hours.

6 You should swallow the tablets whole with water.

7 25 ml to be taken with food.

d) **Mark the above instructions MF (more formal) or LF (less formal).**

Think about why ⌐

Which type of instruction – for medicine or for cosmetics – is more precise and formal? Why?

Summary

- Writers generally vary the level of detail according to what the reader needs to know. In this context, the language of instructions on items that could cause harm is more precise than on other items. The language also tends to be more formal when the writer needs to show that the topic is serious.

- Imperative structures tend to be quite neutral, e.g. *Take two* tablets every two hours.

- Other structures are used where the topic is more formal:

passive + *should*

Two tablets *should be swallowed* whole with water.

passive variation: *(are) to be*

Two tablets *to be taken* before breakfast.

If the object is understood, it can be omitted, particularly in the negative form:

Not *to be taken* with alcohol.

2 Reduced imperatives

a) Match the instructions to the items.

1   Serve cold.

2   Shake thoroughly.

3   Close firmly.

4   Apply warm.

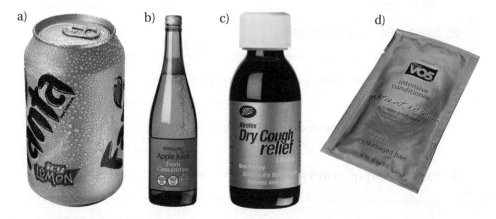

a)   b)   c)   d)

b)   Where would you add the words *the drink, the bottle, the top, the conditioner* into the instructions?

Summary

In instructions on packets and containers of household items, verbs normally considered transitive are frequently found without their objects. The objects are understood from the context.

Shake (the bottle) well. ➤ *Shake well.*

A very common structure therefore is a reduced imperative. These contain just the verb and either an adjective e.g. *serve chilled*, or an adverb of manner e.g. *twist gently*.

Adjectives describe what happens to the noun (*wipe clean* = it becomes clean), or the condition it should be in (*cold, hot, warm*).

Adverbs of manner describe the action. Adverb phrases can also be used in reduced imperatives:

Massage (the cream) <u>into the skin</u>. ➤ *Massage into the skin.*

C Language practice ⌘

1

a) Rewrite the sentences so that they are suitable for instructions on household items.

1   You shouldn't give these tablets to children under twelve.
    ➤ Do not give / Not to be given / Should not be given to children under twelve.

2   You shouldn't eat this cream.
    ....

3   You shouldn't use these painkillers with other drugs.
    ....

4   You shouldn't take more than 12 tablets in 24 hours.
    ....

5   You shouldn't spray this product into your eyes.
    ....

6   If you've already taken 4 doses of a paracetamol-containing product, you shouldn't take this medicine.
    ....

7   You can give these tablets to children under 6, but only if a doctor tells you that it is safe.
    ....

b) Complete the text with the correct form of the verb in brackets.

> ✓ **How to take Paracetamol Caplets 500mg**
> Check that the foil packaging is not broken before first use.
>
> Adults and children over 12: 1 to 2 caplets **a)** .... (take) three or four times a day, if needed, up to a maximum of 8 caplets in 24 hours.
> Children 6 to 12 years: Half to 1 caplet **b)** .... (take) three or four times a day, if needed, up to a maximum of 4 caplets in 24 hours.
> ✗ **c)** .... (repeat / not) **the dose more frequently than every 4 hours.**
>
> **d)** .... (exceed / not) THE STATED DOSE.
>
> **e)** .... (take / not) with any other paracetamol-containing products. Immediate medical advice **f)** .... (seek) in the event of an overdose, even if you feel well, because of the risk of delayed, serious liver damage.

2

a) Look at these reduced instruction forms and correct any mistakes.

1 Pat dryly.

2 Rub in thoroughly.

3 Hold upright.

4 Dissolve complete.

5 Sprinkle lightly.

6 Spray light and even.

7 Rinse clean.

8 Reapply regular.

b) Write instructions for the following. Use the instructions from the previous activity.

1 Sunscreen lotion

   <u>Rub in thoroughly</u> .... and <u>reapply regularly</u> ....
   – at least every hour.

2 Facial cleansing soap

   .... and ....

3 Oven cleaner spray

   .... and ....

4 House plant food granules

   .... and ....
   around the base of the plant.

3 Here are some illustrations showing how to use a window and glass cleaning spray. Write a set of instructions for the product, incorporating reduced imperative forms where appropriate.

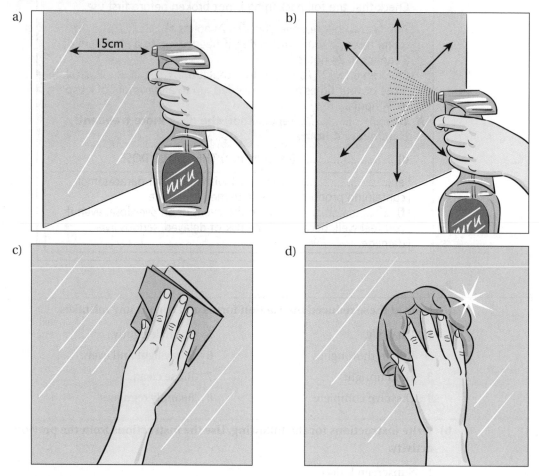

a)

b)

c)

d)

D Follow-up tasks

1 Find instructions for a household medicine and a cosmetic item in your own language.

- Are there similarities with the patterns worked on in this unit? Are the instructions on the medicine clearer and simpler than those on the cosmetic item?

2 Think of a medicine or cosmetic product which you use regularly.

- Write out the instructions for using it.

- Do not mention the name of the item. Show your instructions to a classmate and see if they can guess what the product is.

UNIT 18 Advertisements

Using adverbs for emphasis

Using *only* for focus

A Introduction

1 What is the funniest or most memorable advert you have ever seen?

2 Here is an advertisement from a magazine.

- What is the advert for? What are the innovative features of the product?

Exclusive technology changes the face of make-up.

New. So Fresh.

Multi-dimension make-up.

New ZColor Technology redefines make-up for the ultimate flexibility. *So Fresh* is so flexible, it even moves with your skin to stay flawless and feel comfortable. In two innovative formulas: Liquid Foundation SPF 8 and Loose Powder.

Think about why

A complete sentence contains a main verb. How many complete sentences are there in this advert? What other constructions are used instead of complete sentences? Why is this way of presenting information useful in an advert?

ONE

B Language working in context ⌐⟶

1 Using adverbs for emphasis

a) What effect do the adverbs have on the following sentences?

   1 He sold his guitar.

      He <u>even</u> sold his guitar.

   2 She is happy.

      She is <u>so</u> happy.

   3 The winner was 12 years old.

      The winner was <u>only</u> 12 years old.

b) Two of the adverbs suggest that the writer is surprised, the other is used for simple emphasis. Mark them E for emphasis and S for surprise.

Think about why ⌐⟶

The words *so, even* and *only* show the attitude of the writer. *Even*, in particular, depends on shared understanding between the reader and the writer. In the example above, both need to know something about the owner of the guitar to know the significance of selling it. Why is this kind of link between the reader and the writer useful in adverts?

Summary

The adverbs *so, only* and *even* are very commonly used in advertisements. They emphasise the meaning of the word(s) directly after them.

● The adverb *so* is similar in meaning to *very* and can be used in front of the adjective to make the meaning stronger:

   You look so happy.

● The word *even* also emphasises the writer's point. It suggests the writer is surprised. Shared or contextual information is needed for the reader to understand it:

   Mark even paid for the meal. (The writer and reader are surprised, perhaps because their acquaintance does not usually spend money on eating out.)

● The adverb *only* is used in front of quantities to emphasise smallness and to limit the meaning:

   They promised me an experienced teacher, but he was only a trainee.

c) **Find the adverbs *so* and *even* in the following advertisements. What part of speech is each of the adverbs modifying?**

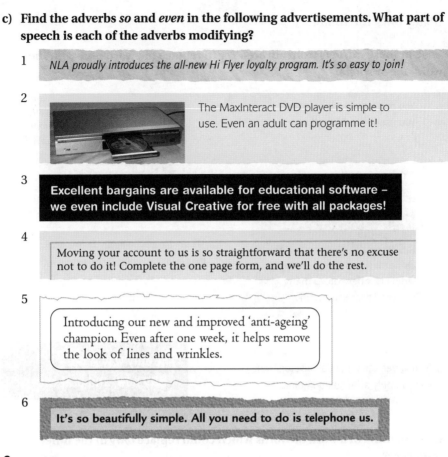

1   NLA proudly introduces the all-new Hi Flyer loyalty program. It's so easy to join!

2   The MaxInteract DVD player is simple to use. Even an adult can programme it!

3   **Excellent bargains are available for educational software – we even include Visual Creative for free with all packages!**

4   Moving your account to us is so straightforward that there's no excuse not to do it! Complete the one page form, and we'll do the rest.

5   Introducing our new and improved 'anti-ageing' champion. Even after one week, it helps remove the look of lines and wrinkles.

6   **It's so beautifully simple. All you need to do is telephone us.**

Summary

- *Even* can be used more widely than *so*. It can modify nouns, prepositional phrases and verbs:

  Even the colours are different. (+ noun)
  Even in cloudy conditions, the film works well. (+ prepositional phrase)
  They even provided breakfast at the meeting. (+ verb)

  When *even* is used to modify adjectives it tends to be in the pattern *not + even + adjective*:

  It's not even expensive.

- *So* is used with adjectives which can show degree:

  The tribute was so special.

  It can be used with passive verbs and adjectives in the pattern *so + passive verb/adjective + that*:

  He was so shocked by the news (that) he fainted. (+ passive verb)
  She was so happy (that) she cried. (+ adjective)

  So can also modify other adverbs, e.g. *very, extremely, unusually.*
  It's so very cheap.

2 Using *only* for focus

a) **Look at these extracts from adverts. Try to replace the word *only* with the word *one* or *single*.**

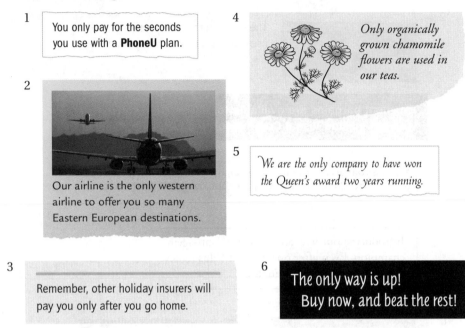

1

> You only pay for the seconds you use with a **PhoneU** plan.

2

> Our airline is the only western airline to offer you so many Eastern European destinations.

3

> Remember, other holiday insurers will pay you only after you go home.

4

> *Only organically grown chamomile flowers are used in our teas.*

5

> *We are the only company to have won the Queen's award two years running.*

6

> The only way is up!
> Buy now, and beat the rest!

b) **Can you think of a word or words which could replace *only* in the other sentences?**

Summary

● *Only* limits the range or scope of the words modified:

Only <u>citizens from the countries listed</u> can apply. (Citizens of other countries cannot apply.)

It can also show how special or unique something is as part of a noun phrase with *the*:

We are <u>the</u> <u>only</u> company that offers free travel insurance as standard. (No other company offers this.)

● *Only* is a very flexible adverb. It can be positioned in front of noun phrases and verbs:

Only a man would think that! (+ noun)
She only laughs at her own jokes! (+ verb)

Only can be used with adjectives in a similar pattern to *even*:

It's not only expensive, (but) it's (also) badly made. (*not* + *only* + passive verb/adjective)

1 **Add the word *so* to the sentences.**

a) We proudly present our new customer loyalty program. Taking advantage has never been easy!

b) What makes our product different? Price, quality, choice.

c) With a patented nozzle, HAIRDOO sprays finely and evenly, you can hardly see it or feel it.

d) We're the only big city bank to offer many little bank services.

e) The make-up is clever! It even moves with your skin to stay flawless and feel comfortable.

2

a) **Look at these extracts from adverts for the following products: a health magazine, an oven, a hotel, an Air Miles scheme. Decide which advert is for which product.**

1 Good food that helps you feast on all your old favourites, ... when you're on a health drive.

2 All our ovens have Powercool, which keeps doors safe to touch, ... during roasting.

3 You'll .... find a championship-quality golf course, if you fancy a round or two.

4 There are countless ways to raise your total .... higher, with the many airlines and service partners participating in the program.

b) **Which adverb could fit in all the gaps? Choose from the following: *so, even* or *only*.**

3 **How many places could you put the word *only* into this wine advertisement? Where do you think it was in the original version?**

Fine Italian wines start with the finest Italian grapes. That's why we choose those kissed by a little more sun. Great with food.

4 You work for the marketing department of a car manufacturer and have been asked to write an advert for a new, small car. Look at the features the manufacturers want to emphasise:

- it is eco-friendly - it uses dual-fuel (electricity and petrol)
- no other car has this system
- it's efficient in cities as well as the open road - it uses less petrol than any other car
- parking is very easy
- it's cute and fun to drive!

'the Bambi'

- Start the advert like this: *The Bambi's so cute, and doesn't cost the earth …*
- Say why the car is unique: *It's the only car to …*
- Say something surprising about the car: *Even in city driving conditions …*
- Explain another good feature: *And parking is …*
- Summarise the good points: *The only thing you have to do is … !*

D Follow-up tasks

1 Write an advert including some of the adverbs worked on in this unit.

- **Here is the advertising brief:**

Project: New campaign to introduce the new VivaMax car.

Background: Manufacturer breaking into luxury car market. Reputation for reliability and performance already established in smaller cars, but brand perceived as dull. Manufacturer wants to build on reputation and increase credibility.

Objective: VivaMax to symbolise power and intelligence

Target audience: managers, ambitious high-flyers

Important details: unique 'intelligent' braking system, comfortable long distance, reliable

2 Look out for *so, even* and *only* (used as adverbs) when you are reading.

- **Make a list of them in a vocabulary notebook. Write down the complete sentence. Analyse what the adverbs tell you about the opinion of the writer.**

UNIT 19 Essays and reports

A Introduction

1 • What advice would you give to someone about how to write an essay or a report?

• Do you have a different approach if you write an essay out of class or one in an examination?

2 Look at this introduction to an essay on a particular form of English.

• Why is there a debate about this style of speaking? ○━━

> Estuary English is a particular way of speaking common in London, the south-east of England and along the Thames Estuary. There has been considerable debate about the term since it was first used in a newspaper article in the 1980s.
>
> Some commentators have focused on Estuary English as a unique form. However, attempts to separate the form from other local varieties have so far been problematic.
>
> In spite of numerous popular studies investigating Estuary English, an agreed definition remains difficult. This is largely due to the fact that professional linguists have been reluctant to investigate a 'form' which has been first described by a newspaper, and which has never been accurately described and defined.

Think about why ○━━

What is the purpose of each of these three paragraphs? Why are they so important to the rest of the essay?

B Language working in context ⌒

1 Comparing approaches

a) Here is part of a research report. What is the researcher interested in?

> The bending mechanisms of metals have been studied both experimentally and through computer modelling using various measures. These include hardness (Brown, 2004), indentation (Hughes, 2005), and compression (Peterson and Li, 2004; Jones et al, 2005).

b) What are the main research methods that have been used in the past?

Think about why ⌒

Why do you need to review previous work and make comparisons about approaches to a topic when you write an essay or a research report?

c) Match the structure of these extracts to the descriptions:

1   Contrasting approaches.
2   Contrasting approaches showing which the writer shares the view of.
3   Contrasting approaches explaining something about the history of the topic.

i)
> Although early research regarded gesture and talk as separate (for example, Clarke, 1993), more recent work regards these as part of the same communicative event (Peters, 2003).

ii)
> Some researchers regard gesture and talk as separate (for example, Clarke, 1993), while others study the two in combination (Peters, 2003).

iii)
> Most researchers have approached gesture and talk as two separate areas of investigation (for example, Clarke, 1993). Surprisingly few have focused on the integration of the two forms of communication (Peters, 2003).

Summary

- The simplest way to introduce two different approaches is to start with the topic and add two adverbs or adverb phrases after an appropriate verb. Typical verbs are *research, study, investigate, analyse, examine, consider*:

  Children's language has been studied (both) quantitatively and qualitatively. (adverbs)

  Children's language has been investigated (both) through quantitative methods and qualitative methods. (adverb phrases)

  Alternatives to *through* are:
  by, via, by means of

- Another way to present different approaches is to show how methods or ideas have changed over time. You will need a clear opening sentence which tells the reader that you are contrasting approaches through time:

  During the 1980s, [X] was investigated mainly by interviews with patients. (Give some examples, including references here.) *However, in the late eighties and for the next 15 years, statistical modelling became common.* (Give examples, including references here.)

- You can show the ideas that are closest to yours or that you agree with most by using an opinion adverb. Common opinion adverbs are *surprisingly, interestingly, predictably, naturally, obviously, astonishingly* (strong).

  Surprisingly, little research has focused on [X], *although work has been done on* [Y].

2 Making your own point and supporting it with references

a) Match the content to the extract.

1 Data from air samples.

2 Evidence from developmental psychology.

3 Analysis of texts.

a)
> Many quantitative studies into the effects of pollution in the major cities of developing countries have been carried out (Bennet, 1989; Holdridge, 1996; Caspers, 2000; Stephens, 2004).

b)
> Research articles (RAs) have received extensive attention in genre analysis (Berkenkotter and Huckin, 1995; Brett, 1994; Hopkins and Dudley-Evans, 1988).

c)
> Children develop their understanding of the world through play (Piaget, 1970).

b) Which two examples provide a review of previous work? Why is the other example different?

c) **Here are three different ways of incorporating other people's ideas into your writing. Look at the names and dates in brackets and answer the following questions: Why are the names of the authors inside the brackets in 2 and 3, but not in 1? Why is there a page number in 3 but not in 2?**

1   Chafe (1982, 1991) has investigated the typical features that impart qualities of orality and literacy to texts …

2   … a $9m^2$ sample of square configuration had previously been shown to be optimal (Wade and Ladewig, 1982).

3   More work is needed on the influence of social factors in language development. In particular, Battle et al note the need to '… distinguish between those aspects of linguistic variation that represent the diversity of the English language from those that represent … disorders (Battle et al., 1984, p24).'

Summary

There are three main ways you can put other people's work in your own writing:

- Supporting a statement by a reference at the end of a clause

  If you do not use references, a statement is just your opinion.
  Parks in cities improve people's lives. (your opinion)
  Parks in cities improve people's lives (Hubbard, 2004). (Your opinion is the same as Hubbard's, and Hubbard has done some research on the topic.)

  Writers also use references at the end of clauses to generalise about the background to their own work. This is usually in the form of several studies, all on the same topic, or using the same approach:

  Several studies have shown that parks in cities improve people's lives (Brown, 1999; Jones, 2001; Lim et al, 2003; Hubbard, 2004).

  This shows the level of background knowledge of the writer, and confirms their right to 'speak' on the topic – they have read enough!

- Using the author as a subject

  This is useful when you want to focus on one particular study.

  Gale (2002) reported that on average European males were taking four fewer days' holiday than the previous generation.

- Direct quotation

  'Turn-taking in spontaneous speech is at the same time the simplest and the most complex of mechanisms (Hughes, 2005: 37).'

  If you are just reporting facts discovered by someone else, do not use a direct quotation. Use direct quotations only when the original language adds something to your discussion.

  ~~*Gale (2002, p443) reports that 'the European male is taking 4 days fewer holiday than the previous generation.'*~~ ✗

C Language practice 🔑

1

a) Combine the following descriptions of approaches. Replace the verb *research* with one of these verbs: *study, investigate, analyse, examine.*

1   Improvements to toxic waste disposal have been researched in Britain. Improvements to toxic waste disposal have been researched in France.

   → Improvements to toxic waste disposal have been investigated both in Britain and in France.

2   This method of irrigation has been researched in China. This method of irrigation has been researched in Egypt.

3   The effects of schooling on criminal behaviour has been researched experimentally. The effects of schooling on criminal behaviour has been researched through qualitative methods.

4   Bird migration patterns have been researched via direct observation. Bird migration patterns have been researched via satellite technology.

b) Comment on whether you can use all the verbs in all the sentences. Describe any changes in meaning if different verbs are used.

2   **a) Here are three sets of notes made by a research student about the main ideas of three articles. What is the topic of the research articles? Which article discusses the topic in the most general way? Which article looks at two different languages?**

Article 1:
Kranmaer, John (2004). 'Turn-taking as rational behaviour', Journal of Social Sciences. 21/4. pp65-97.

... says that turn-taking is part of a 'fundamental survival mechanism' (p95), not just learned social behaviour – study based on 12 married couples ...

Article 2:
Hooper, Edgar (2001). 'Mother-child interactions as indications of learned turn-taking behaviour', Journal of Ethnographic Research. 12/1. pp20-49.

... says that children learn to take turns at a very early age, perhaps 18 months ...

Article 3:
Chen, Ying (2003). 'A multi-cultural approach to analysing turn behaviour', Language and Social Studies. 30/2. pp78-90.

... says that Chinese and British turn-taking is quite different, suggests more work from a multi-cultural perspective is needed – first study of its kind ...

b) **Add the correct references in the right place in these sentences. Look back at the notes for the previous activity to help you.**

1) A great deal of work has been carried out on turn-taking behaviour.

2) Turn-taking is learned behaviour.

3) It has been argued that more work is needed on turn-taking from a variety of perspectives.

3

a) **Here are some notes made by a student on different approaches to solving traffic congestion and examples of solutions these approaches suggest. Can you add any items to the list of examples?**

> (1) 'additional capacity' proposed and strongly supported by Charters (2002) -- more roads = less congestion, he says.
>
> Example: build more roads
>
> (2) making people change their habits - defined by Hobson (2003) as 'travel demand modification (p9)' - same number of people travel, but in a way that means fewer cars.
>
> Example: encourage people to share their car
>
> (3) reducing the need to travel - Cross (2004) calls it 'travel demand reduction' (p167) - particularly wants more home-workers.
>
> Example: raise the road tax

b) **Write an opening section to an essay comparing these approaches. Include the three approaches, with references and some examples.**

D Follow-up tasks

1 **Find an introductory textbook to a subject you are familiar with.**

- ● Look for passages where there are references to other work. Categorise these according to whether they are supporting a statement by the writer, describing several different studies, giving a direct quotation from the source, or other.

2 **Find an academic article and analyse the language used in the introduction.**

- ● Underline any places where methods, approaches, or concepts are compared. Does the writer use any of the patterns described in this unit?

- ● Try to write your own version, using a topic you are familiar with.

Interesting the reader and changing the focus using *it*

Adjectives and verbs commonly used in *it* clauses

A Introduction

1 ● Do you read any monthly or weekly magazines?

 ● Which part of a magazine do you always read first?

2 Look at this extract from an article about women's careers.

 ● What does the word *it* refer to in the final sentence?

You know when you have made a good decision. You know that when you study for a certain subject or pursue a career, it's because you feel passionately about it, which is what makes the following figures so upsetting. A report this year from the Department of Trade and Industry (DTI) revealed that there are 50,000 women science, engineering and technology (SET) graduates not working in their respective industries at any one time. … It's a criminal waste of talent and skills. But why is it happening?

Think about why

The above extract from a feature article contains this sentence: *You know that when you study for a certain subject or pursue a career, it's because you feel passionately about it … .* The writer could have said: *You study for a certain subject or pursue a career, because you feel passionately about it.* Why did the writer use the more complex sentence?

1 Interesting the reader and changing the focus using *it*

a) Underline the word *it* in the following extracts.

1

When the magnificent Richard's House started serving lunches last spring, it instantly became the place for the foremost families of Barbados to meet. One of the oldest plantation houses in the Caribbean (built in 1635), it is filled with antiques and surrounded by 3.5 acres of gardens.

2

Whether it's your first time or your 50th, the magic of flying to the Caribbean in winter, swapping British cloud for tropical pleasure, is one of the all-time travel experiences.

3

It may not be the most exciting thing you buy when you redesign your bedroom, but your mattress is the key to a good night's sleep.

b) Circle the topic that each *it* refers to. In which extract(s) does the writer use *it* to refer back to a topic already mentioned? In which extract(s) does the writer use *it* to refer forwards to something?

Think about why 🔑

Look at the third extract again. Why does the writer delay the topic by beginning the paragraph with *it*? What does this force the reader to do?

Summary

It can be used to refer back to previous items. These can be specific nouns, ideas, or general topics:

The interior design is wonderful. It makes other apartments look old-fashioned.

It can also be used to refer forwards:

When it opened in 2001, the hotel was an immediate success.

When *it* refers back to something, this is called *anaphoric reference*. When the topic is delayed and *it* refers forwards, it is known as *cataphoric reference*.

c) Look at the underlined sentences in these two extracts. Decide whether the references are anaphoric or cataphoric.

1 (From an article about why criminals commit crimes.)

At school in the 1930s, everyone was poor but some of my friends had nice homes – I wanted to be like them. <u>It was about a year after I left school that I started stealing</u> – I got a buzz out of it at the time. I never became a bank robber or a con man – I just remained an ordinary thief.

2 (From an article about a famous British politician who lost a lot of weight.)

… he continued eating three full meals a day – a household routine of breakfast, lunch and dinner. <u>It was the meals that changed</u> – with no fat, dairy products, buttery sauces, sugar, fried or carbohydrate food or alcohol allowed. By following this method, the 64-year-old former Minister lost about a pound and a half a week, going from 17st to 12st in less than a year 'without too much difficulty'.

d) The underlined sentences begin with *It was …* . What effect does this have?

Summary

Writers can use *it* for emphasis as well as for linking backwards and forwards.

● These emphatic sentences are created by taking a basic sentence and introducing the part you want to focus on with *It + be*.

Her attitude shocked me.
<u>It was her attitude</u> that shocked me!
(*It + be* + focus of the sentence + *that* + clause)

The word *it* does not really refer to anything. It fills the place of the subject. This use is sometimes called a dummy subject.

● Different parts of a base sentence can be moved into focus:

The weather was disappointing.
➤ *It was the weather that was disappointing.* (focus = subject)

He's broken his leg.
➤ *It's his leg that he's broken.* (focus = object)

I met him first in New York.
➤ *It was in New York that I first met him.* (focus = adverb)

2 Adjectives and verbs commonly used in *it* clauses

a) **Read the following extracts. It would be possible to remove the words in bold. Why has the writer used them?**

1

Kevin Keegan must have seen in his mind's eye the haunted, hunted images of former England football managers as he considered accepting the FA's[1] offer of the full-time post.

It's obvious that an army of friends, and even other professionals certainly did. And they tried hard to persuade him against accepting the job.

2

Scientists knew before the Fifties that the Earth's magnetic pole varied slightly from year to year, but only then was it discovered that the magnetic field periodically reverses.

It's claimed that there have been 171 reversals over 76 million years, but it's not known why this happens.

b) **The words in bold look similar in both extracts, but they follow different patterns. Match the patterns to the extracts:**

   i) *it* + *be* + verb past participle + *that*

   ii) *it* + *be* + adjective + *that*

Summary

A large number of evaluative adjectives and verbs are used with *it*. They either express the attitude of the writer or the writer's level of certainty about facts. There are two patterns:

- *it* + *is/was* + adjective + *that* + clause

  It was remarkable that she was elected. (expressing attitude)
  It is probable that he was murdered. (expressing level of certainty)

  Further examples of adjectives you can use with *it* in this way are:

  Attitude: *arguable, clear, fascinating, incongruous, interesting, ironic, obvious, odd, paradoxical, remarkable, strange, surprising, true, understandable*

  Certainty: *(far from) certain, (in)conceivable, (un)likely, (im)plausible, (im)possible, (im)probable*

- *it* + *is/was* + verb past participle + *that* + clause

  It is anticipated that there will be a merger next year. (expressing probability)
  It was alleged that the boss stole the funds. (The writer may not agree, therefore this verb shows her attitude.)

  Further examples of verbs you can use with *it* are:
  accept, argue, assert, assume, believe, claim, envisage, expect, say, suggest

---

[1] *FA = Football Association*

C Language practice 🔑

1

a) Put these mixed up paragraphs in order.

1

a) is its least practical:

b) perhaps the kitchen's most striking feature, however,

c) and was chosen by the couple for its appearance and not really to bring in any extra light.

d) the curved glass wall that was already in place before work on the kitchen began,

2

a) seems to them to incorporate the very best in quality.

b) over the past 22 years,

c) although it's in complete contrast to what the Wilsons have grown used to

d) their new house

b) Which paragraph contains anaphoric reference and which contains cataphoric reference?

2 Rewrite these sentences without *it*.

1 It was a year later that I visited New York for the first time.
   → I visited New York for the first time a year later.

2 It was when he moved to Greece that Benson found inspiration for further novels.

   ....

3 It was the shorter working hours which attracted her to the job.

   ....

4 It is the location which is the main factor in house sales.

   ....

5 It is never the poor who gain from tax cuts.

   ....

6 It might be the colour of the carpet which is wrong.

   ....

3 Rewrite these sentences starting with *it*. Put the focus on the part of the sentence that is underlined.

a) They moved house <u>last year</u>.

    → *It was last year that they moved house.*

b) The Robinsons moved <u>to Wales</u>.

....

c) <u>The article about nuclear power</u> was published in the New Scientist.

....

d) The central bank raised the interest rates <u>to cut inflation</u>.

....

e) <u>The personal tax rates</u> will all rise next year.

....

f) He was famous for <u>his ability to remember a great many facts and repeat them</u>.

....

4 You are a journalist. Here are some notes you have made for a new feature article. Write the opening paragraph making it as attractive to the reader as possible. Incorporate at least one construction using *it*.

> Camping moves into the 21st Century!
> Very different from 30 years ago. Used to be uncomfortable, unfashionable, unpopular.
> Equipment makes the difference - tent design = better, and fabric has changed = warmer (new high tech canvas), and in great colours.
> Really surprising -- Even rock stars and fashion designers camping out under the new high tech canvas!

D Follow-up tasks

1 Write the opening sentences of a magazine article on your favourite hobby or sport.

● If you are working in class, don't mention the name of the hobby or sport. Show it to a classmate and see if they can guess what it is.

2 Find three short feature articles from magazines or online 'lifestyle' sites.

● Analyse the uses of *it* you find. Underline and categorise the different uses: backward linking, forward linking, focus / emphasis, comment with adjective / verb or something else!

● Can you add to the list of verbs and adjectives that can be used with *it* clauses?

Answer key

Unit 1 Everyday notes

A

1
- People write notes when they have to give information or instructions to someone who is not present.
- You might need to leave a note for a business contact you are meeting at a conference or leave a note on someone else's car if you damage it! The main difference between notes to friends and to strangers is not formality, but how much shared information you have.

2   a)   printer (W)
      To tell the technician where to move the printer.
    b)   inside front door (H)
      To remind yourself to buy milk.
    c)   manuscript (W)
      To explain where the reader needs to look in a manuscript.
    d)   desk (W)
      To confirm a meeting with a colleague and make a joke.
    e)   kitchen door (H)
      To prevent someone hurting themselves on broken glass on the floor.

Think about why

Because the writer knows that the note will be thrown away, they do not write very carefully, or worry about punctuation and grammar.

Notes naturally contain the minimum words for the message to be clear. People writing notes leave out words, use contractions, shortened forms of words and other standard abbreviations.

B

1   Shortening the message by using ellipsis

a)   1, 2, 4, 5, 6, 7, 9 should all be marked X.

b)   Rang Peter
      → I rang Peter. (The subject / first person pronoun has been left out.)
      Might be back around 7.
      → I might be back around 7 o'clock. (The subject / first person pronoun has been left out.
      7 o'clock has been shortened to 7.)
      Mo'hd sending the files on Friday.
      → Mohammed is sending the files on Friday. (The auxiliary verb has been left out. The person's name has been shortened.)
      Am leaving tonight.
      → I am leaving tonight. (The subject / first person pronoun has been left out.)
      Will e-mail my arrival time.
      → I will e-mail my arrival time. (The subject / first person pronoun has been left out.)
      Couldn't find keys. Taken yours.
      → I could not find my / the keys. I have taken yours. (The subject / first person pronouns and *the* have been left out. *Couldn't* is a contraction. Auxiliary verb *have* left out.)
      Transfers from airport arranged with Michael Evans.
      → Transfers from the airport have been arranged with Michael Evans.
      (The auxiliary verbs and *the* have been left out.)

c) 1 Yes, as long as the meaning is clear.
  2 Yes (see sentences 4 and 9), but take care that the meaning is clear.
    Leave in the auxiliary verbs *be* and *have* if you think the reader might be confused.
    They help to show whether a missing subject is singular/plural or a verb phrase is active/passive.
  3 No, you cannot omit modal auxiliaries.

Think about why

Notes to family and friends will be different from notes to other people. You share a great deal of background knowledge with your friends and family and can often shorten the message because of this.

2 Common abbreviations and when to use them

a) 1 dets= details, asap = as soon as possible
  2 Fri = Friday, a.m. = morning
  3 ext = extension
  4 fax = facsimile message, no. = number
  5 figs = figures, ie = that is, Oct = October, Jan = January
  6 docs = documents, e.g. = for example
  7 NB = remember
  8 P.S. = and another thing

b) 1 CU = See you!
  2 CU2NITE = See you tonight.
  3 CUL8R = See you later.
  4 WAN2CU = I want to see you.
  5 GR8 = great
  6 RUOK? = Are you OK?
  7 YRUL8? = Why are you late?
  8 NE MSG? = Any message?
  9 XLNT = excellent
  10 RNG B4 U GO = Ring before you go!

C

1 a) (Am) posting report Mon
  b) (Am) finishing first draft today
  c) correct
  d) correct
  e) John might ring / John rang
  f) Can't / Couldn't read your writing!
  g) correct
  h) Sally delayed. Will start the meeting on my own.
  i) correct

2 a) 'cos or cos
  b) bet or betw
  c) b'day
  d) Xmas
  e) cttee
  f) enc
  g) fwd
  h) info
  i) mth
  j) no
  k) poss
  l) tel
  m) w/e or w'end
  n) yr (*year* is also shortened to *yr*)

3 a) Pls inc comparative sales figs for another area, e.g. Northern branches.
  b) Will have report re tax situation by Weds.
  c) NB Read this b4 the meeting!
  d) Will send info asap.
  e) (There's been) (a) power cut all pm, i.e. couldn't make dinner! Let's eat out!
  f) (There've been) 3 urgent faxes.

D

1 Suggested answer:
  Jenny rang (401379). Can you ring her? She's out between 2 and 3.

Unit 2 Greetings cards

A

1 open discussion questions

2 a) retirement   b) illness   c) passing an exam

Think about why

It is possible to buy cards that have the message already printed because there are a variety of conventional expressions used in English for different occasions.

B

1 Conventional expressions used for different occasions

a)

1	Christmas	6	New Year
2	birthday	7	illness
3	wedding anniversary	8	birthday
4	bereavement[1]	9	Christmas
5	a happy event (e.g. passing a test, getting engaged, getting a job)	10	birthday

Think about why

Leaving out words makes messages more informal. Shortened messages are not always appropriate for serious occasions, such as illness or bereavement, as they may seem too casual.

b)
1 I hope you are well / to see you soon / all is going well.
2 Wishing you a speedy recovery / you were here.
3 Hoping you are well / to see you soon / all is going well.
4 Best wishes
5 I wish you were here. (*I wish to see you soon* is possible, but the meaning of *wish* + *to* is closer to *want* and is not used in this way in greetings. *I wish you a speedy recovery* is possible, but sounds old fashioned.)
6 Hope you are well / to see you soon / all is going well.

2 Varying the warmth and formality of the message

a) Yours sincerely (F), Yours faithfully (F), Yours truly (F)

b)

Best wishes (N)	Regards (N)
Love (N), (W) (informal)	Thinking of you (W)
Much love (W)	Kind regards (N), (W) (formal)
Lots of love (W)	With all my love (X)
Love from us all (W)	

c)
1 Hope you're well.
2 Hope to see you soon.
3 Wishing you every happiness.
4 Sincere best wishes
5 Congratulations from all the team. / Congratulations!
6 Sincere condolences on your loss.

d) Card 1
The greeting *Darling* is very informal, but the message is very formal. If you were writing to a close friend you might write:
Darling,   *Congratulations!!*   *Love, [nickname]*

---

[1] a *bereavement* is the death of a close relative or friend

If you were writing to a work colleague you might write:

Dear [first name]

Congratulations!

Regards, [first name]

You might also add a comment about the event here, e.g. *I was delighted to hear about your promotion.*

Card 2

This card is for a bereavement. The language of the message is too informal and the use of exclamation marks very inappropriate. Even if you are close, the language in this kind of card will be formal. For example:

Dear Joan,

I am thinking of you. / My thoughts are with you.

Love (to close friends or family) / *Best wishes* (to others)

C

1   a)   iv   b) ii   c) i   d) iii   e) v

2   a)   *Wishing* you a Happy New Year.   d)   *Wish* you were here.
    b)   *Hoping* to see you soon.   e)   *I hope* you have a lovely day.
    c)   *Hope* you are better.

3   a)   Happy Christmas!   e)   ✓
    b)   Happy New Year!   f)   Good luck!
    c)   Get well soon   g)   Many happy returns
    d)   ✓   h)   Congratulations!

4   Possible answers:
    a)   Happy Birthday. Best wishes, Rebecca
    b)   Get well soon!! Lots of love, R xx
    c)   Happy retirement. Kind regards, Rebecca (Hughes)

D

1 and 2 open tasks

Unit 3 Formal letters and e-mails

A

1   open discussion questions

2   This e-mail is from an estate agent. The agent is asking the reader to visit the website to see a new property for sale. They are also asking them to update their personal information.

Think about why

The most polite part of the e-mail is: *If you wish to benefit from these, please log in and select the 'silver service' option. We would be grateful if you could take a moment to re-confirm your personal profile at the same time.* The style is more polite because the writer is asking the reader to do something which may be inconvenient.

B

1   Expressing requests for action and making suggestions

a)   This e-mail is an automatic response to an enquiry from a website. It is not possible to guess what the enquiry was.

b) The underlined clauses are examples of conditional forms.

As an automatic response, this e-mail has to fit any enquiry. Therefore, the writer has to try to guess what the reader might want to do or know. The writer uses a conditional form to do this: *If you need to contact us about your original message, please quote the tracking number above.*

The writer also uses a conditional form to make a suggestion of something the reader might want to do: *If you would like to know more, please click on the link given below.*

c) 1 = changing a ferry reservation

Please change your reservation as soon as possible. (direct request)

2 = a problem with a financial matter, possibly a bank account

Please contact me urgently on 0124 347767 concerning your account. (direct request)

3 = a hotel reservation

The writer makes an indirect request: *If you could give us a credit card number, we will reserve.*

Think about why

(Please) give us a credit card number. Using an imperative is much more direct, but could be considered impolite.

2 Combining modals and conditionals to make requests

a) 1 d   2 b   3 c   4 e   5 a   6 f

b) 1, 2 and 5 are the easiest tasks; 3, 4 and 6 are the most difficult. The difficult tasks are preceded by the conventional forms *We would be very grateful* or *If you could possibly … .* The easier tasks just use *If + present simple* or *If you could … .*

C

1   Suggested answers:

    a) If you require more information, please fill in your details below.

    b) If you require free virus protection software, please download it from our website.

    c) If you receive a request for your account details and password, please ignore it and contact us immediately.

    d) If you could send us a daytime contact number or e-mail address, we will comfirm when the new account is 'live'.

2

a)   1   (!) As this is an urgent request, it is probably also unexpected.

    2   (✓) As the reader requested the form, they will be expecting to complete it.

    3   (✓) As the reader has already been reminded about this, they will be expecting to have to pay it.

    4   (!) It can be difficult and time-consuming gathering these documents.

    5   (✓) This is easily done.

    6   (!) It can be difficult and time-consuming gathering these items.

b)   Possible answers:

    We would be grateful if you could telephone urgently.

    Please complete the enclosed form.

    Please pay the bill within 10 days.

    We would be extremely grateful if you could send in documents to confirm your identity.

    Please click on the link and it will automatically update your security settings.

    If you could possibly send your passport and a separate photograph of yourself, we would be very grateful.

3 Possible answer:
Dear [first name, family name]

Packed with lots of exciting new features, the Fly4fun website is even better than before! Just give us a couple of minutes of your time and you could access a great new world of offers.

If you could take a moment to re-register on the site, we would be grateful. Please follow the simple instructions to change the security settings at the same time.

If you have a special trip planned in the coming months, you might be interested in visiting the site to find out more about special promotions.

Regards,
The Fly4fun sales team.

D

1 and 2 open tasks

Unit 4 **Policies and agreements**

A

1 ● open discussion question
   ● Obligatory (in UK): car insurance, buildings insurance (if you have a mortgage), software licence. Strongly recommended: travel insurance.

2 ● modal forms: might, must
    Must expresses obligation.
   ● try = endeavour; keep = adhere

Think about why

Policies and agreements are formal documents and have a particular legal status. Therefore, the language is generally authoritative and the vocabulary is highly formal. *Endeavour* and *adhere* are examples of more formal vocabulary.

B

1 Modals and semi-modals of obligation

a) *must* and *should* are used to express strong obligation:
   … *convictions <u>should</u> be fully declared …*
   … *you <u>must</u> ensure that any information … has been stated on your form.*
   You <u>must</u> do this immediately …
   … *you <u>must</u> contact us within three working days …*

b) *Have to* is close in meaning to both forms, but because it is less formal sounding, it would not replace them in these contexts.

2 Formal versus informal language choices

a) 1 and 4

b) The following phrases are particularly formal:
   in the unlikely event that
   should occur
   subsequently cease to
   in consequence
   be obliged to
   reserve the right to

c) *Be required to* and *be subject to* have a similar meaning to *must.*
All new customers <u>*are required to*</u> …
Accounts still outstanding … <u>*are subject to*</u> immediate termination.
Virtual servers … <u>*will be subject to*</u> immediate deactivation.
Be prohibited from has a similar meaning to *must not.*
You <u>*are prohibited from*</u> sending unsolicited bulk mail messages.

Think about why

It is useful for the writer because the focus is on the reader's obligation. The reader cannot question the authority of the 'hidden' subject!

C

1 a) You must not take money out of the country.
     (*You should not take money out* is also possible, but is slightly less strong.)
  b) You do not have to sign until you have legal advice.
     (*You need not sign* is also possible, and is slightly less strong.)
  c) You should not lend your car to another driver.
  d) You must sign by the end of the month.
     (*You should sign* is possible, but less strong. *You have to sign* is also possible, and is less formal.)
  e) You should let the insurer know if you change job.
     (*You need to let the insurer know* is also possible, and is less formal.)
  f) You must not hold a non-European account.
     (*You should not* is also possible, but is less strong.)

2 a) provided that = if   b) on expiry of = after   c) in the event that = if

3 a) vi   b) viii   c) i   d) ii   e) iii
   f) v   g) ix   h) iv   i) vii

4
a) 1   The guarantee doesn't apply.
    2   No, the guarantee expires after four years.
    3   Yes, you will have to pay labour costs.
    4   No, these are free of charge.

b) Suggested answer:
    Faulty parts will be replaced free up to four years after you buy the product. You will have to pay labour costs. You have to send in your guarantee card within 14 days of buying the product.

D

1 ● Possible answer:
   Customers must agree to the following rules:
   A deposit of £100 must be paid in advance.
   You are required to return the boat within 3 hours.
   You are expected to return the boat undamaged.
   Passengers should check that they have all their belongings when they leave the boat.
   All passengers should be able to swim, and children under the age of 15 must wear a life jacket at all times.

2 open task

Unit 5 Business letters

A

1   • People write business letters about impersonal topics, such as money or contracts.
    • open discussion question

2   This is a letter of reference recommending Ms Ferrer to a potential employer.

Think about why

This is a convention in formal business letters. It gives the main topic of the letter.
Re: means *regarding* or *on the topic of.*

B

1 Patterns of noun phrases

a) 2, 3, 5, 7, 1, 4, 6
Dear Sir/Madam,
Re: problem with a fridge-freezer
I am writing to complain about the fridge-freezer which I bought from your store.
On 20th February, I bought a Gold Star fridge-freezer from you for £750. This machine is faulty as the handle on the freezer has broken.
I wish to reject the goods and claim a refund. Please respond to my complaint within seven days.
Yours faithfully,
Angela Hardy

b) problem with a fridge-freezer
the fridge-freezer which I bought from your store
a Gold Star fridge-freezer
the handle on the freezer

c) noun + prepositional phrase:
problem with a fridge-freezer
the handle on the freezer
noun + clause:
the fridge-freezer which I bought from your store

Think about why

Noun phrases giving factual information will be more common.

d) 1   To family lawyer   5   To family lawyer
    2   To property landlord   6   To an organisation with a job vacancy
    3   To estate agent   7   To an organisation with a job vacancy
    4   To family lawyer

e) 1   start (main noun), of divorce proceedings (prepositional phrase)
    2   payment (main noun), of rent (prepositional phrase)
    3   particulars (main noun), of 19 Lovedale Road (prepositional phrase)
    4   will (main noun), in name of Mr H Sayed (prepositional phrase)
    5   claim (main noun), for compensation on behalf of Mrs J. Jones (prepositional phrase)
    6   request (main noun), for further details and application form (prepositional phrase)
    7   information (main noun), about the post of headteacher at Margrave School (prepositional phrase)

The prepositional phrases for 4, 5 and 7 have a further noun phrase inside them: *name, compensation, post* and *headteacher* are also nouns with prepositional phrases after them!

2 Writing opening statements

a) 1 to request

2 regarding / with regard to

b) The first statement is about an action: requesting an estimate.

C

1 a) Re: Policy no. 678-978-HP

(The word *insurance* would probably not be necessary if you were writing to the insurance company.)

b) Re: Job details, ref. PG/107/B

(*Ref* is the conventional abbreviation for *reference*.)

c) Re: Application procedure

d) Re: Invoice no. 1009/8

(*no.* is the conventional abbreviation for *number*.)

e) Re: tenancy agreement for Flat 4, 76 Park Road

f) Re: letter of complaint

2

a) and b)

Possible answers:

1 I am writing to request further job details. (N)

2 I am writing regarding an insurance policy. (N)

3 I write to query a tenancy agreement. (MF)

4 I am writing with regard to the application procedure. (N)

5 I am writing about an invoice. (LF)

6 I write regarding a recent letter of complaint. (MF)

3 Suggested answer:

Dear Sir/Madam,

Re: Further information for vacancy ref TX771 (driving instructor)

I am writing to request further information and an application form for the above vacancy.

Yours faithfully,

Rachel Hughes

D

1 and 2 open tasks

Unit 6 Hobby books

A

1 open discussion questions

2 ● painting or oil painting

● only = just

… *just three primary colours.*

… *just from the three basic ones.*

sufficiently = enough

When you think the colour is dark enough …

Think about why

Colour is uncountable when it refers to the concept (abstract noun). When referring to different colours of the spectrum, the noun is countable, e.g. *Mixing two primary colours produces a secondary colour.*

B

1 Using articles with countable and uncountable nouns

a) Out of context these nouns would be listed as typically:
potato (countable)
flour (uncountable)
dough (uncountable)
moisture (uncountable)

b) <u>potato</u> gnocchi (uncountable)
455 g cooked mashed <u>potato</u> (uncountable)
230 g plain <u>flour</u> (uncountable)
Mix the <u>potato</u> and <u>flour</u> (uncountable)
a kneadable <u>dough</u> (countable)
More or less <u>flour</u> (uncountable)
the amount of <u>moisture</u> (uncountable)
in the <u>potatoes</u> (countable)
Knead the <u>dough</u> lightly (countable)

Think about why

It depends on how the writer is thinking about the noun.

c)
1	carrot	2	tarragon	3	the carrots
4	the butter	5	the cream	6	the sugar

2 Degree adverbs

a) Instruction 1 relates to the picture.

b) exactly = just
as much as necessary = enough
nearly = almost

C

1   a) carpentry: hammer C, wood U, nails C, drill C, saw C, glue U, varnish U
b) sewing: needle C, cloth U, thread U (could be C), scissors C, pattern C, thimble C, iron C

2   a) <u>Pasta</u> with b) <u>Lemon</u> Sauce
Peel off c) <u>the zest</u> of one lemon, and put it in d) <u>a frying pan</u> with
e) <u>the butter</u>. Cook gently for 5–10 minutes without letting f) <u>the butter</u> burn. Remove g) <u>the zest</u>.
Add h) <u>the cream</u>, grate in i) <u>the zest</u> of
j) <u>the second lemon</u>, and cook until you have k) <u>a well-flavoured cream</u>.

3   c, a, b, d

4   a) To grow herbs in containers make sure the pot is large <u>enough</u> to give all the requirements they need when fully grown.
b) Heat the milk until it <u>almost</u> boils. (*Heat the milk almost until it boils* is more common in spoken English.)
c) Saw through the plank to <u>just</u> half-way.
d) Sketch the outline first, so that it can <u>hardly</u> be seen, in case you make a mistake.
e) Whisk in <u>nearly</u> all the cream.
f) Bring the two sheets of metal together until they are <u>barely</u> touching.

1 and 2 open tasks

Unit 7 Informal letters and e-mails

A

1   open discussion question

2   a) and e), b) and g), c) and f), d) and h)

Think about why

When people know one another they write informally: they shorten words, use lots of slang and use punctuation that wouldn't be found in formal published writing, e.g. exclamation marks. They also leave out details which they both already know.

B

1 Using articles to show shared knowledge

a)   1= a meal   2 = a football match   3 = a wedding   4 = a new home

b)   The reader and writer are referring to something they both know about already.

c)   1   <u>Breakfast</u> is different in <u>England</u>. <u>People</u> eat <u>cereal</u>, fried or grilled <u>meat</u> (such as <u>bacon</u> or <u>sausages</u>) and <u>eggs</u>.
      2   On <u>Sunday</u>, the breakfast was really horrible. The eggs were cold and the coffee was too weak.
      3   <u>Breakfasts</u> were generally fine, but nothing like <u>home</u>!

d)   The articles reflect the generality of the statements. 2 describes one particular breakfast so *the* is used before *breakfast*, *eggs* and *coffee*. In 1, the writer is describing the meal in very general terms, and so no article is used: *breakfast*. In contrast to both, in 3 the writer is describing several actual meals, perhaps on a holiday, and uses the plural form.

2 Handling vague language

a)   going to the gym: stuff, things, kit
      eleven-hour flight: stuff, things, belongings
      mending a car: tools, stuff, things

b)   stuff, things

c)   Extracts 1 and 3 are accompanied by attachments.

d)   i)   1 these = the photos   iii) 2 that = menu
      ii)   3 this = the menu   iv) 4 that = going this weekend

Think about why

E-mails are a bit like a conversation. You could say *Here is the* ... to someone as you hand them something and this is echoed in the e-mail. Because short personal e-mails are similar to conversation, and often contain the first e-mail in the reply, you don't have to explain everything in detail, so the use of *this* and *that* to refer to familiar topics is common.

C

1   a)   the letter   b)   a photograph   c)   a car   d)   the car

     e)   the flowers   f)   the man   g)   a man   h)   flowers

2

a)   1   a   2   d   3   e   4   b   5   c

b)   1   things / stuff / belongings (formal)

     2   stuff / things / bits and pieces

     3   thing / stuff

     4   stuff / things / bits and pieces

         (Use *bits and pieces* with care as it may make the items sound unimportant.)

     5   equipment / stuff / things

3   a)   Yes, this is fine.

     b)   These are different from the original document.

     c)   This is excellent news!

4   Possible answers:

     a)   Thanks for this. I look awful!

     b)   Thank you for these. Here are the contact details I promised you.

     c)   Thank you for these. They will be very useful.

     d)   Thanks, but I can't find the attachment. Could you re-send? (As the attachment isn't there, you can't refer to it.)

D

1 and 2 open tasks

Unit 8 Catalogues

A

1   open discussion questions

2   a)   ii (watering cans)   c)   iv (garden storage boxes)

     b)   iii (kitchen weighing machine)   d)   i (lamp)

Think about why

The maximum information needs to be compressed into each phrase or clause, so these texts have high levels of complex noun phrases.

The texts contain positive language, mainly adjectives, which aims to attract the reader to the item being sold.

B

1   Building noun phrases using *for* and *with*

a)   1   for   2   for   3   with   4   with   5   for

b)   1   d   2   a   3   e   4   b   5   c

     6   h   7   f   8   g

c)   *With* links the main noun to other features of the same item.

     For links the main noun to other items or activities.

Think about why

Phrases using *with* are like adding a relative clause with *have* but are simpler and shorter. As space in catalogues is limited, they are often used in this context.

2   Adjectives which take prepositions

a)
1   A perfect meal for two.
2   This folding table is very convenient for entertaining outside.
3   These chocolates are excellent with coffee.
4   A mobile phone charger that is suitable for most types of phone.
5   This is a handy tool for cutting metal.
6   This black scarf will be perfect with any coat.
7   A watch with a second hand is an ideal present for a sportsman.

b)   *Perfect* can be used with both *for* and *with*. In the example *This black scarf will be perfect with any coat*, it means that they go together well. In the example *This folding table is very convenient for entertaining outside*, it means that it is very good in a particular situation.

C

1
a)   A patterned towel with a fish design on the borders.
b)   A wide-brimmed yellow hat for keeping the sun off your face.
c)   A white sarong with pink flowers.
d)   A parasol with a red stripe pattern.
e)   A lovely yellow beach bag for carrying your swimming things.
f)   A natural citrus spray for preventing insect bites.

2
a)   perfect, ideal, just the thing, excellent <u>with</u>
b)   perfect, ideal, just the thing, excellent <u>for</u>
c)   perfect, ideal, just the thing, excellent, handy, convenient, suitable <u>for</u>
d)   perfect, ideal, just the thing, excellent <u>with</u>
e)   perfect, ideal, just the thing, excellent, suitable <u>for</u> (*Handy* and *convenient* are not possible here because the focus is on how the object looks, not what you can do with it.)

3
a)   1 b   2 d   3 c   4 a

b)   open task

D

1 and 2 open tasks

Unit 9 Technical manuals

A

1   open discussion questions

2   a) is for a general reader, b) is for an expert user or technician

Think about why

Texts written for an expert assume that they have specialised knowledge and that things do not need to be explained. The language is more impersonal and, in particular, the vocabulary is more technical. There are also complex noun phrases with very specialised meanings, e.g. *radial clamping system*.

B

a) Most of these nouns have more than one meaning and many everyday words can be used in a technical context with a very different meaning.

In this text, the underlined words have the following meanings:

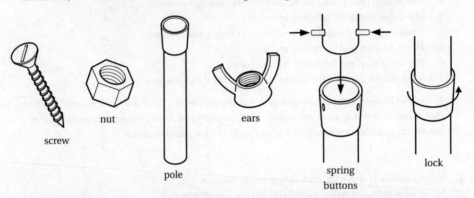

screw

nut

pole

ears

spring
buttons

lock

b)

article	Standard adjective	Pre-modifying noun(s)	Adjective from a verb	Main noun
the	–	–	holding	screw
–	–	thumb	–	nut
the	black	nylon, pole	–	tip
the	–	–	–	ears
the	two	spring	–	buttons
the	–	pole	–	lock

c) tip (4 words: the black nylon pole tip)

Think about why

In technical writing the pre-modifying words are factual rather than evaluative. This is because the language needs to be very precise, and the opinion of the writer is unimportant.

d) fibreglass, steel, plastic, nylon, brass, alloy, metal

e) 1 fibreglass handle insulator   4 double solenoid valve
   2 plastic corner connector   5 LED display window
   3 steel retaining spring

f) These adjectives would come first.
   1 black fibreglass handle insulator
   2 circular plastic corner connector
   3 lower steel retaining spring
   4 rectangular LED display window
   5 small double solenoid valve

2 Prepositions used to express precise actions

a) Examples 2, 4 and 5 are from a technical manual. The others are from a general household manual.

b) 1A   2PP   3A   4PP   5PP   6A

C

1 a) a 20 cm plastic tube
   b) circular fibreglass insulator
   c) front cover hinge

   d) red plastic cable
   e) lower section fixing lock

2

a) This text actually comes from a general instruction manual, but is quite technical in its description. Position the car seat onto the Surefix base (1) so that the locking catches on the car seat fit over the attachment bars of the base (5). Push firmly down until the catches on the seat engage. Rotate the handle of the car seat forwards into the 'Fitting' position, see page 3 for more information (2). Wrap the diagonal portion of the vehicle seat belt webbing around the back of the car seat (6). Thread the diagonal section of the vehicle safety belt through the webbing slot in the rear of the car seat backrest (4). Pull the diagonal section of the vehicle seat belt in the direction shown in figure (3) to remove all of the slack so that the car seat is held firmly against the vehicle seat.

b) pre-modified nouns: the car seat, the Surefix base, the locking catches, the attachment bars, the 'Fitting' position, the diagonal portion, the vehicle seat belt webbing, the diagonal section, the vehicle safety belt, the webbing slot, the car seat backrest, the vehicle seat belt, the vehicle seat

   prepositional phrases: onto the Surefix base, on the car seat, over the attachment bars of the base, until the catches on the seat engage, of the car seat, into the 'Fitting' position, for more information, of the vehicle seat belt webbing, around the back of the car seat, of the vehicle safety belt, through the webbing slot in the rear of the car seat backrest, in the direction shown in figure [x], against the vehicle seat.

3

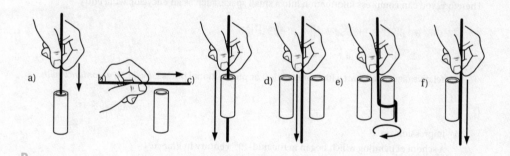

a)   b)   c)   d)   e)   f)

D

1 and 2 open tasks

Unit 10 Encyclopaedias

A

1 open discussion questions

2 ... *whose* works ... are largely based on Czech folk themes
   Whose refers to Leos Janacek.
   ... *which* he directed until 1920.
   Which refers to the college.

Think about why

The main function of these texts is to provide facts. The writer does not have to express their opinion, and does not have to attract, interest or persuade the reader to do anything. The reader already wants to find the information. Therefore, the writer can compress a great deal of information into complex sentences, often adding relative clauses relating to main nouns.

B

1   Defining and non-defining relative clauses

a)   brick: (ceramic structural material) which is made by pressing clay into blocks and firing them in a kiln.
(Bricks,) which in their most primitive form were not fired but were hardened by being dried in the sun, have been used for thousands of years.

… and (the ancient races) who occupied this region may have been the first users of brick.

In (Babylonia,) where there was a lack of both timber and stone, the thick clay deposited by the overflowing rivers was the only material adaptable to building.

b)   The clauses giving definitions are: *which is made by pressing clay into blocks and firing them in a kiln*, and *who occupied this region*. There is no comma before these. The other two clauses give additional information and are punctuated between commas.

Think about why

These clauses are useful to a writer because you can add information without starting a new sentence. Therefore, you can compress information into a small space, such as an encyclopaedia entry.

2   Starting a relative clause with a preposition

a)   1 b   2 d   3 a   4 c

b)   The relative clauses all start with a preposition or prepositional phrase: *by, in, in accordance with*.

C

1   a)   impressionism
A school of painting which began in the mid-19th century in France.

b)   aeroplane
Fixed-wing aircraft, which is heavier than air, and is supported by the dynamic reaction of the air against its wings.

c)   Holbein, Hans (1497 – 1543)
A painter, born in Augsburg, Germany, the son of Hans Holbein, who was also a painter of merit.

d)   insects
Members of the *phylum Anthropoda*, whose bodies are divided into three parts and have six legs.

2   a)   BORON
A hard, non-metallic solid, which as a pure element does not occur free in nature. It forms many compounds in which it is bound to oxygen.

b)   BUDDHISM
A central belief is the law of karma, by which good and evil deeds result in appropriate reward or punishment in this life or in a series of rebirths.

c)   CANKER
(botany) A general term for a disease of plants, *in which bark formation is prevented; typically caused by bacteria or fungi.*

d)   MORSE CODE
System through which it is possible to communicate using long and short sounds in particular patterns which represent letters.

3   a)   automated teller machine (ATM)
         The formal name for the 'service tills' now common outside most banks and building societies,
         <u>through</u> which money can be withdrawn and other transactions carried out.
     b)   cornett
         The cornett has been revived in modern times for performing older music including Bach's
         cantatas, <u>in</u> which it often doubles the highest voice part.
     c)   pitcher plant
         Any of the members of three separate families of carnivorous plants, <u>in</u> which the leaves are
         modified to form lidded pitcher traps containing water and enzymes.

4   Suggested answer:
     Helicopter
     Type of aircraft in which lift from the ground is obtained by horizontal propellers called rotors. When
     the rotor of a helicopter turns it causes a reaction in the body of the helicopter which causes it to
     spin. To compensate for this, many helicopters have a second rotor which is positioned near the tail
     of the aircraft.

D

1 and 2 open tasks

Unit 11 Blurbs

A

1   open discussion questions

2   ● It's from a thriller.
    ● John Corey was wounded. The opening six words gives this information: *Wounded in the line of
      duty …*

Think about why

These texts are meant to attract the reader and make them want to buy the book. They are a kind of
advertising text. The space is very limited, so the writer needs to pack information into a small space.

B

1   Adding information at the start of a clause

a)   The sentence is difficult to read because all the background information (her life before Ellen went to
     London) is put between the main focus (*Ellen*) and the main verb (*is thrown*).

b)   Brought up in an isolated community in the Scottish Highlands where reading any book except the
     Bible on Sunday was forbidden, Ellen May Peters is suddenly thrown into the exciting world of
     London in the 1880s when her parents die and she is taken to live with her rich aunt.

Think about why

There is not much space available so information is packed into the sentences. These texts are full of
densely packed noun phrases, with high levels of noun pre-modification. Sometimes a whole story is
compressed into a sentence. One way of doing this is to put some information at the start of the clause in
front of the subject.

c)   1 a   2 e   3 b   4 c   5 f   6 d

d)   The words in italics relate the states or beliefs, the words in bold relate to actions.

2 Variations in noun pre-modification

a) 1 a romantic novel, 2 a detective novel, 3 a spy thriller

b) 1   childhood (noun), innocent (adjective)
   2   unpopular local (adjectives), popular (adjective), view (noun)
   3   innocent (adjective), Czech (adjective)

C

1   a)   Fired by his employers after he was accused of stealing from them, but now the head of the largest investment bank in Europe, Peter Sterling decides …

   b)   Shot while preventing an armed robbery and now living in a small village in the south of France, Chicago detective Ronny Hale soon realises …

   c)   Once owned by a Contessa suspected of having committed three murders, and sold to the multi-millionaire businessman Orlando Wei for the highest price ever paid for a building in Europe, the Palazzo D'or reveals …

2   a)   Wounded in the jungle, our hero managed to walk 50 km to safety.

   b)   Thought to be in France, the criminals were really in America.

   c)   Separated from his parents at the age of 2, Jean-Paul was finally reunited with his family at the age of 35.

   d)   Sold into slavery and never taught to read or write, Kita Mara eventually escaped, gained an education and wrote her gripping life story.

   e)   Suspected of spying and found guilty, Jane Peterson spent 10 years trying to prove her innocence.

   f)   Rescued by the gentle people of the planet Zar, and told by them the secret of eternal youth, Pete Lee was questioned by the FBI on his return to Earth.

3   On a remote <u>island</u>, a wealthy <u>entrepreneur</u> secretly creates a theme park featuring living <u>dinosaurs</u> created from prehistoric DNA. Before opening it to the public, he invites a top palaeontologist and his paleobotanist <u>girlfriend</u>, a renowned mathematician, and his two eager <u>grandchildren</u> to experience the park. But their visit is anything but tranquil as the prehistoric <u>predators</u> break out and begin hunting the island's human <u>inhabitants</u>.

4   a)   A dramatic and deeply moving love story.

   b)   A secret disease research laboratory.

   c)   A passionate but shy (or shy but passionate) young woman.

   d)   A laugh-a-minute comedy drama.

   e)   A fast-moving action thriller.

5   Suggested answer:

   Stolen by the famous female burglar, Madam Xara, and hidden in the collar of her pet cat, the extremely rare and beautiful 'rose petal' diamonds are finally recovered after a thrilling chase across three continents.

D

1 and 2 open tasks

Unit 12 Holiday brochures

A

1   open discussion questions

2   a) *** b) **** c) **

Think about why

You can use a word like *or*, *and*, or *but* to create a list in a sentence. This process is called co-ordination. You can see it in the second sentence of each hotel extract in part A.

Lists are common in brochures because brochure texts do not provide complex information. They aim to provide a list of attractive features and useful facilities.

B

1   Expanding the sentence using co-ordination

a)   1   c and a   2   b   3   d

Think about why

The units that are co-ordinated need to be the same grammatically (noun + noun, adverb + adverb, clause + clause), so that the sentence can function smoothly. This is because they are added into the sentence as two equal items and taking one away would still leave a grammatically correct sentence.

b)   1   This charming, traditional hotel offers <u>a refined style</u> and <u>comfortable guest rooms</u>.
    2   The <u>elegant lobby</u> and <u>impressive guest rooms</u> are ideal for today's traveller.
    3   <u>Original marble stairs</u> have been polished and <u>layers of paint</u> removed to reveal beautifully detailed ironwork dating from 1902.
    4   <u>Guests receive a complimentary continental breakfast</u> and <u>will enjoy microwaves, refrigerators and coffeemakers in their suites</u>.

c)   1   i   verb (<u>offers</u>) + object + *and* + object
    2   iv   subject + *and* + subject + verb (*are*)
    3   ii   subject + verb (*have been polished*) + *and* + subject + verb (*removed*)
    4   iii   subject + verb (*receive*) + object + *and* + (subject) + verb (*will enjoy*) + object

2   Handling adjective choices

a)   Suggested answers:
    1   inelegant, scruffy
    2   old-fashioned, classical
    3   modern, contemporary, up-to-date
    4   large, big, well-sized, spacious
    5   dark, dull, dim, gloomy
    6   inadequate, poor, mediocre
    7   uncomfortable
    8   bare, simple, modest

b)   You would be most likely to find positive adjectives in a brochure, e.g. *large*, *big*, *well-sized*, *spacious*. You would also find adjectives which could be positive or negative depending on the customer, e.g. *old-fashioned*, *contemporary*, *modern*, and adjectives which put less positive aspects in a better light: *modest*, *simple*.

c)   spacious (F/E), new (F), comfortable (E), large (F/E), two (F)

C

1

a)   Located right off the prestigious Champs Elysées Avenue, at the crossroads of (fashion, entertainment <u>and</u> business), the legendary luxury four-star Sasha Champs Elysées radiates an incomparable charm which has seduced an (elegant <u>and</u> international) clientele. (The hotel's décor is inspired by nature, <u>and</u> the team of staff are dedicated to service.) (Hotel Sasha offers the chance to experience the very best of Paris life, <u>and</u> gives the (business <u>or</u> holiday) traveller a feast of (traditional services <u>and</u> modern facilities).)

b) and c)

    prestigious (E), legendary (E), luxury (E), four-star (F), incomparable (E), elegant (E), international (E/F), hotel's (F), very best (E), business or holiday (F), traditional (E/F), modern (E/F)

2   Original text:

Sasha Champs Elysees is a magical place where your every whim is within reach and the amenities are unparalleled. Savour a delicious meal at the hotel restaurant. Immerse yourself in the scene at Sasha's lounge bar: it redefines casual chic.

3   a)   and internet connection   b)   and Spanish

    c)   and an executive floor   d)   and congress

4   Possible answer:

The hotel Brava has 150 air-conditioned rooms with hairdryer in room, mini-bar, and room service. The hotel is ideal for families as it has babysitting, doctor-on-call, games room, laundromat, and a heated pool.

D

1 and 2 open tasks

Unit 13 Travel guides

A

1   open discussion question

2   The city being described is London.

    a)   London   b)   English   c)   London   d)   Thames

Think about why

Yes, they will be different. Travel books try to both interest and inform the reader. Holiday brochures try to attract and sell. Encyclopaedias aim to inform. A description in a travel guide book will be more lively and less factual than one in an encyclopaedia.

B

1   Adding information to the noun by apposition

a)   1 c   2 a   3 b

b)   Yes, these words could be removed and you would still have a complete sentence with a subject, verb and object. These phrases add more information about the opening noun.

c)   1 b   2 a   3 g   4 e   5 d   6 f and c

d)   Phrase b is different because it contains a word referring back to the main opening noun: *its*.

Think about why

Apposition is very common in guide book writing because it allows background information about a main topic to be added very flexibly and keeps the style quite light. Using apposition can break up sentences which might otherwise be boring! It also means that you can add information without starting a new sentence, so it is useful when space is a consideration.

2   Varying the style by moving appositional phrases

a)   … the country's capital …

    … with its bars and clubs …

    … the fascinating old town built in the 13th century …

b)   Stockholm, the country's capital, is remarkably peaceful despite having a population of 1.6 million. With its bars and clubs, Stockholm is a progressive city, though there are pockets which have a village feel. A good place to begin to explore is Gamla Stan, the fascinating old town built in the 13th century.

c)   The rewritten text reads better and was in fact the original published text.

C

1 a)   ▲ Edinburgh only became Scotland's capital … / Edinburgh ▲ only became Scotland's capital …
   b)   ▲ Dublin is home to many students. / Dublin ▲ is home to many students.
   c)   The modern capital of Italy is Rome ▲.
   d)   ▲ London is still an important centre for trade./London ▲ is still an important centre for trade.
   e)   Here on Java we find the largest Buddhist Temple in the world ▲.

2 a)   Although most of the visitors head for the beaches of Cancun, a major resort city in the northeastern part of the Yucatan, many others visit the area for its many Mayan archaeological sites.
   b)   Recognised as the 'Pearl of the Orient', Penang Island, a fabulous destination, is renowned for its superb beaches and exotic sights.
   c)   Created in the 17th Century by Kobori Enshu, the genius of Zen landscape, the garden of Dembo-in is the best-kept secret in Asakusa.

3 Suggested answers:

Version 1
Madagasgar, an island in the Indian Ocean, is a nature lover's dream. Cut off from the African mainland for millions of years, Madagascar has types of animals and plants preserved that are found nowhere else in the world, and you can see all these in a spectacular collection of accessible national parks.

Version 2
Located in the Indian Ocean and cut off from the African mainland for millions of years, the island of Madagascar has types of animals and plants preserved that are found nowhere else in the world and is a nature lover's dream. You can see all these in a spectacular collection of accessible national parks.

Version 3
With its spectacular collection of accessible national parks, Madagascar, an island in the Indian Ocean, is a nature lover's dream. Cut off from the African mainland for millions of years, Madagascar has types of animals and plants preserved that are found nowhere else in the world.

D

1 and 2 open tasks

Unit 14 Direct mail

A

1 open discussion questions

2 most exciting = most thrilling, less difficult = easier or simpler, more pleasant = nicer, highest quality = finest

Think about why

A letter is better way of selling things than an advertisement in a magazine because it addresses the reader directly and personally.

B

1 Adding comparative and superlative structures to the sentence

a) 1 a charity
   2 a magazine

3 a mobile phone company
4 a hotel company

b) 1 better future
   2 most important 60 minutes

3 bigger discount
4 most extensive and cheapest range

Think about why

Advertising language contains many comparatives and superlatives because it is trying to show how special the product is and how it is different from competing products and the 'top' product.

The writer may choose to leave out the second noun because then they do not have to be specific about exactly what their products are cheaper, better or more attractive than!

c) 1 a or b   2 d   3 a or b   4 c

2 Adjectives that do not normally take comparative or superlative forms

a) Use *better* to complete this text. *Perfect* is an adjective with absolute meaning and is not normally used in comparative or superlative forms.

b)

adjective	comparative	superlative
good	better	best
perfect	(not possible)	(not possible)
acclaimed	more acclaimed	the most acclaimed
beautiful	more beautiful	the most beautiful
global	(not possible)	(not possible)
favourite	(not possible)	(not possible)
exclusive	more exclusive	the most exclusive
unique	(not possible)	(not possible)
unrivalled	(not possible)	(not possible)

C

1 a) <u>the quickest and most popular way</u>
    b) <u>higher discounts</u>
    c) <u>latest, and</u> … <u>most comprehensive</u> … <u>brochure</u>
    d) <u>the greatest photographers and writers</u>
    e) <u>Bigger, better, brighter</u>.
    f) our <u>best</u> (<u>competition</u>)

2 Hint: try putting *very* in front of the adjective. If this is not possible, then the adjective doesn't have a comparative or superlative form either.

    a) yes (redder, the reddest) b) not usually c) yes (more popular, the most popular)
    d) no e) no f) yes (more spacious, the most spacious) g) yes (farther or further, the farthest or the furthest) h) no i) yes (more dramatic, the most dramatic) j) no

3 a) higher   b) lower   c) lowest
    d) better   e) highest   f) tastiest

4

a) and b) Suggested answers:

    It couldn't be easier to apply. (a credit card)
    No one gives you more benefits. (health insurance)
    There is nothing more challenging. (doing an MBA)
    Driving to work couldn't be more fun. (car)
    It couldn't be more fun. (ferry)

D

1 Possible answer:
Bartree is changing. You'll be surprised next time you look. Brighter colours, funkier designs, the cutest skirts and tops ever. You'll still find the quality you expect from us, but now we're offering this together with the most stylish, the most eye-catching and the sexiest designs ever.

2 open task

Unit 15 Everyday instruction booklets

A

1 ● open discussion question
● The more complex or unusual the item, the more likely it is to need a full instruction book. However, even simple equipment, such as a kettle, will have a booklet.

2 installing, using, connecting, dialling

Think about why

-ing forms focus on actions so they are common in instruction booklets since these explain tasks which the reader needs to carry out.

B

1 Non-finite clauses: *-ing* and *to* …

a) 1 C   2 E   3 F   4 E   5 E   6 F   7 C

b) 1 To set the temperature, turn the dial in a clockwise direction.
2 To grill meats, switch on the grill function.
3 To adjust the time, press the buttons marked H and M.
4 To change the light bulb, ensure the appliance is switched off and remove the old bulb.
5 To clean the interior, switch off the appliance and wash with a damp cloth.

Think about why…

-ing forms are often used as headings because they express a complete action.

c) and d)
1 shaking out SIM   2 using SIM   3 turning SIM
4 No *-ing* form. SEQ

e) *-ing* forms are used to express simultaneous actions.

2 Prepositions introducing *-ing* clauses

a) 1, 2 and 4 refer to the refrigerator; 3 refers to the coffee machine.

b) after, before

C

1 a) Installing the battery / the shelves / the monitor / the telephone line.
b) Connecting the telephone line / the battery / the monitor.
c) Adjusting the volume / the shelves / the time / the strength / the brightness / the monitor.
d) Changing the volume / the time / the battery / the strength / the brightness. (Here the meaning of *change* is similar to *adjust*.)
e) Assembling the shelves.

2   a) after   b) when   c) by   d) when   e) when   f) before / when

3   How to make perfect espresso coffee
     a) Open the hinged lid, unscrew the water tank cap <u>by turning</u> it anti-clockwise.
     b) Lift and turn again to remove the cap.
     c) To <u>fill</u> the water tank use your glass carafe to measure the volume of water required.
     d) Always <u>switch</u> the machine off and remove the plug from the socket before <u>filling</u> (or <u>you fill</u>) the
        water tank.

4   a) Turning   b) To turn   c) pressing   d) enter
     e) entering   f) Making   g) To unblock

D

1 and 2 open tasks

Unit 16 Newspaper stories

A

1   open discussion questions

2   A scientist who tried to blackmail food companies by threatening to poison their products was jailed
     <u>for three years (time) yesterday (time)</u>.

     Brown was arrested <u>in Vienna (location)</u> <u>last month (time)</u> as he tried to withdraw a £50,000 first
     instalment from a bank in the city.

     <u>Yesterday (time)</u> Brown told the court <u>in Vienna (location)</u> that he devised the plan after the failure of
     a computer firm he ran.

Think about why

The reader also wants to know when and where the story happened. This means that news stories have
very high levels of adverbs, and adverbial phrases, giving information about time and location. Using
them also allows the writer to put a lot of information into a small space.

B

1   Handling and combining adverbs of time and place

a)   1   on Sydney (L), yesterday (T), towards the suburbs (L) (direction)
     2   into Manila bay (L) (direction), early today (T)
     3   in Brussels (L), last week (T), in Amsterdam (L), next June (T)
     4   by November (T) (duration), ahead of their summit (T), in Dublin (L), in December (T)
     5   on the website (L)

b)   When both time and place adverbs are used in a sentence, generally <u>location</u> comes before <u>time</u>.

c)   In (ii) the adverbs and adverbial phrases are positioned after the objects / complement.

Think about why

Putting the adverbs in front of the subject makes the writing more vivid. It puts the focus on the
background information – when and where something happened. Writers can use it to delay a topic, or
vary the style.

2 Adverb phrases starting with prepositions

a) All the prepositions (*after, following, amid*) could be replaced with *because of*.

C

1 a) Heavy snow fell in London yesterday.
   b) A plane carrying 150 passengers and crew crashed just 15 minutes after take-off.
   c) The kidnappers were arrested after the release of the victim.
   d) The pound fell sharply against the dollar amid news of the Prime Minister's resignation.

2 a) ▲ the London Stock Market fell sharply again, …
      The London Stock Market fell sharply again ▲, …
   b) … after fears of further corporate scandals ▲ sent share prices crashing.
      … after fears of further corporate scandals sent share prices crashing ▲.
   c) ▲ a survey by the Department of Trade …
      A survey by the Department of Trade ▲ …
      … the rate of growth in activity in the service sector fell back ▲.
   d) ▲ there was some lifting of the gloom.
      There was some lifting of the gloom ▲ .
      The Dow Jones index ▲ …
   e) ▲ predictions that the Bank's Monetary Policy Committee will leave …
      … will leave rates at four per cent hardened ▲.

3 with = alongside
  Ella … has already taken part in fashion shows *alongside* supermodels Naomi Campbell, Kate Moss and Jodie Kidd …
  about = over
  Debate continued today *over* proposals …
  because = after
  His predecessor resigned *after* the bank lost $243m …

4 Possible answers:
  A passenger train hit a goods train just outside Penning Station yesterday morning …
  or Two trains crashed near Penning Station yesterday morning …

D

1 and 2 open tasks

Unit 17 **Packaging**

A

1 open discussion questions

2 Directions: The tablets <u>should be swallowed</u> whole with water. <u>Do not chew</u>.

How much to take: Adults and children over 12: 2 tablets <u>to be taken</u> every 4 hours. <u>Do not exceed</u> 8 tablets in 24 hours. Children 6 – 12 years: 1 capsule every 4 hours. <u>Do not exceed</u> 4 capsules in 24 hours.

Think about why

You need directions for two kinds of everyday products: those that may cause harm if they are used incorrectly (e.g. medicines), and those that have not long been in common daily use. So, perfume does not usually come with instructions because it is such a well-known item, but a more recent product, such as hairspray, will.

B

1 Various styles of instructions

a) perfume (C)
powdered milk (F)
washing powder (CM)
jelly (F)
cough mixture (M)
antiseptic cream (M)

bleach (CM)
facial cleansing cream (C)
lipstick (C)
painkillers (M)
eggs (F)
disinfectant (CM)

b) 1 M   2 C   3 C   4 M   5 M   6 C

c) and d)

1 Active (LF)	2 Passive (MF)	3 Passive (MF)	4 Passive (MF)
5 Active (LF)	6 Active (LF)	7 Passive (MF)	

Think about why

Instructions on medicines are more precise than those on cosmetics. This is because they are taken internally, or may have a strong effect if used incorrectly. As a result, the language tends to be more formal and the instructions more accurate.

2 Reduced imperatives

a) 1 a   2 c   3 b   4 d

b) Between the first word and the second word, e.g. *Serve the drink cold.*

C

1

a) 1 Do not give / Not to be given / Should not be given to children under twelve.
2 Not to be eaten. / Not to be / Should not be taken internally.
3 Do not use / Not to be used / Should not be used with other anti-inflammatory drugs.
4 Do not take more than 12 tablets in 24 hours.
5 Do not spray / Not to be sprayed / Should not be sprayed into eyes.
6 Do not take if you have already taken 4 doses of a paracetamol-containing medicine.
7 Do not give to children under 6 without medical advice. / Not to be given / Should not be given to children under 6 unless advised by a doctor.

b) a) should be taken / are to be taken
b) should be taken / are to be taken
c) do not repeat
d) do not exceed
e) do not take
f) should be sought

2

a) 1 pat dry
2 ✓
3 ✓
4 dissolve completely
5 ✓
6 spray lightly and evenly
7 ✓
8 reapply regularly

b) 1 Rub in thoroughly and reapply regularly at least every hour.
2 Rinse clean and pat dry.
3 Hold upright and spray lightly and evenly.
4 Dissolve completely and sprinkle lightly around the base of the plant.

3 Possible answer:
Hold upright about 15 cm from the surface and spray lightly/sparingly but evenly. Wipe off immediately/at once with a soft, dry cloth or paper towel. Finally, for sparkling results, polish with a clean, dry cloth.

D

1 and 2 open tasks

Unit 18 Advertisements

A

1 open discussion question

2 The advert is for make up (foundation). The product is innovative because it is flexible and moves with your skin.

Think about why

There are only three complete sentences in this text:

Exclusive technology <u>changes</u> (main verb) *the face of make-up.*

New ZColor Technology <u>redefines</u> (main verb) *make-up for the ultimate flexibility.*

So Fresh <u>is</u> (main verb) *so flexible … comfortable.*

The rest of the text is made of adjectives (e.g. *new*), noun phrases (e.g. *multi-dimension make-up*), or the prepositional phrase (*in two innovative formulas*).

These incomplete sentences are very useful in an advertisement because they allow the writer to focus directly on positive features of the product.

B

1 Using adverbs for emphasis

a) These adverbs make the sentences more emphatic and help to show the attitude of the writer to the topic.

b) 1 S   2 E   3 S

Hint: If you want to check, try replacing the words with *very*. Only the adverb used for emphasis can be replaced by this word.

Think about why

Writers of adverts want to connect with a reader and interest them. Using language which shows shared opinions or beliefs is one way of doing this.

c) 1   so easy (*so* + adjective)

2   even an adult (*even* + noun)

3   we even include (*even* + verb)

4   so straightforward (*so* + adjective)

5   even after one week (*even* + prepositional phrase)

6   so beautifully simple (*so* + adverb modifying an adjective)

2 Using *only* for focus

a) You can replace *only* with *one* or *single* in sentences 2, 5 and 6.

b) just, merely

C

1 a) so easy   b) so different   c) so finely and evenly

    d) so many   e) so clever

2

a) 1   a health magazine   2   an oven   3   a hotel   4   an Air Miles scheme

b) even

3   In the original advertisement the word *only* appeared as follows:
That's why we <u>only</u> choose those kissed by a little more sun.

This is a very flexible adverb, however. *Only* could be put quite reasonably in the following positions:
▲ Fine Italian wines ▲ start with ▲ the finest Italian grapes. That's why we choose ▲ those kissed by a little more sun. ▲ Great ▲ with food.
However, the following versions would be a little odd used in an advertisement because they are not positive: *Only great with food. Great only with food.*

4   Possible answer:
The Bambi's so cute, and doesn't cost the earth. It's the only car to protect your pocket and the environment at the same time with its unique dual-fuel system. Even in city driving conditions you will save. And so will the atmosphere. And city parking is effortless. The only thing you have to do is get in and let the fun begin!

D

1 and 2 open tasks

Unit 19 Essays and reports

A

1   open discussion questions

2   Because it is difficult to define.

Think about why

The first three paragraphs introduce the main topic of analysis and give the background to it. If the main topic of analysis is not clear, then your arguments will also not be clear. You need to indicate how you see a problem or topic before going on to make your own argument.
Paragraph 1 defines the main topic (Estuary English) and the problem (debate about it).
Paragraph 2 explains the problem in more detail. Paragraph 3 summarises the present position, and gives some reasons for it.

B

1   Comparing approaches

a) the bending mechanisms of metals

b) experimentation and computer models

Think about why

You need to show that you have read the background to the topic. You also need to show that you understand the topic by putting the ideas or approaches into different categories and comparing them. If you are writing a research-style report, you also need to put your work into the context of other work.

c) 1   ii)   2   iii)   3   i)

2 Making your own point and supporting it with references

a) 1 a   2 c   3 b

b) The example about child development is different because the reference simply supports a statement by the writer. The focus is not so much on the previous work as the point this writer wants to make.

c) In extract 1 the name of the author is part of the grammar of the sentence. If you leave out the name, then the sentence does not have a subject. In the other examples the references are grammatically separate from the clause.

There is a page number in 3 because this is a direct quote and the specific location of the words needs to be given.

C

1

a) Possible answers:
1 Improvements to toxic waste disposal have been investigated both in Britain and in France.
2 This method of irrigation has been investigated both in China and Egypt.
3 The effects of schooling on criminal behaviour has been analysed both experimentally and through qualitative methods.
4 Bird migration patterns have been examined both via direct observation and satellite technology.

b) All the verbs are possible in all the sentences. The meanings are slightly different. If you *analyse* or *study* something the focus is strongly on the main subject as a whole. If you *investigate* or *examine* something the focus is slightly more on the effects or results.

2

a) The topic is turn-taking in conversation. Article 1 is the most general. Article 3 looks at two different languages.

b) 1 A great deal of work has been carried out on turn-taking behaviour (Kranmaer, 2004; Hooper, 2001; Chen, 2003).
2 Turn-taking is learned behaviour (Hooper, 2001).
3 It has been argued that more work is needed on turn-taking from a variety of perspectives (Chen, 2003).

3

a) Possible examples:
Approach 1: create wider roads
Approach 2: free buses
Approach 3: allow more people to work from home

b) Possible answer:
In recent years many solutions have been put forward to solve the problems of traffic congestion. These can be put into three main categories. The first of these is simply to make more road space available. This means building more roads or creating wider roads. The system as a whole has a higher capacity and congestion is lowered (Charters, 2002). A second approach has been called 'traffic demand modification' (Hobson, 2003: 9). In this approach drivers are encouraged to use their cars differently, for example, sharing a car or taking a free bus. Both these approaches mean the same number of journeys are made. There has been surprisingly little work in the area of really reducing demand, for example, by making it easier for people to work at home (Cross, 2004).

D

1 and 2 open tasks

Unit 20 **Feature articles**

A

1   open discussion questions

2   Women not following the careers they had trained for.

Think about why

The simpler version is more neutral and impersonal in style. Using *it* in this way puts a strong focus on the second part of the sentence. Also, using *you know* … makes the writing talk directly to the reader. Feature articles use structures such as these to personalise topic areas and appeal directly to the reader.

B

1   Interesting the reader and changing the focus using it

a) and b)

1   … *it instantly* … / … *it is filled*… (Both refer back to Richard's House.)

2   *Whether it's* … (Refers forward to flying to the Caribbean.)

3   *It may not* … (Refers forward to your mattress.)

Think about why

If you introduce a topic with *it*, you make the reader read a little more actively. In magazine writing this structure is frequently used. It attracts the reader by delaying the main topic. The readers are made to think for themselves about the idea which is going to be introduced.

c)   These uses are a special kind of forward linking (cataphoric reference).

d)   *It was* … is used for emphasis.

2   Adjectives and verbs commonly used in *it* clauses

a)   They are used to introduce comment clauses. These give an evaluation or other indication of the writer's attitude. Adding them changes the sentences from statements of fact.

b)   1   ii   2   i
(*Obvious* is an adjective. *Claimed* is the past participle of a verb.)

C

1

a)   1   b, a, d, c
     2   c, b, d, a

b)   The first paragraph contains anaphoric reference (*its = the kitchen's*)
The second contains cataphoric reference (*it's = their new house*).

2   1   I visited New York for the first time a year later. (or A year later I visited New York for the first time.)

2   Benson found inspiration for further novels when he moved to Greece. (or When he moved to Greece, Benson found inspiration for further novels.)

3   The shorter working hours attracted her to the job.

4   Location is the main factor in house sales. (or In house sales location is the main factor.)

5   The poor never gain from tax cuts.

6   The colour of the carpet might be wrong.

3 a) It was last year that they moved house.
   b) It was to Wales that the Robinsons moved.
   c) It was the article about nuclear power that was published in the New Scientist.
   d) It was to cut inflation that the central bank raised the interest rates.
   e) It will be personal tax rates that will rise next year.
   f) It was for his ability to remember a great many facts and repeat them that he was famous.

4 Possible answer:
   Camping moves into the 21st Century!
   It's amazing. Thirty years ago camping was uncomfortable, unfashionable and unpopular. Today, even rock stars and fashion designers are camping out under the new high tech canvas. It's the equipment that makes the difference. Tent design is better, fabrics are warmer, and they come in a great new range of colours!

   Possible alternative opening:
   Thirty years ago it was uncomfortable, unfashionable and unpopular. Today, even …

D

1 and 2 open tasks

Glossary

Abbreviation / contraction

An **abbreviation** is a shortened form of a word, e.g. *birthday* → *b'day*.
A **contraction** is a shortened phrase, e.g. *have not* → *haven't*.
An apostrophe (') is used to indicate where something is missing.

Adverb / adverbial phrase

The adverbial part of a sentence gives information about how an action is done. This can be in the form of single word **adverbs** (e.g. *carefully*), or **adverbial phrases** that describe an action (*with a smile*, *towards the East*).

Antonym

Word with opposite meaning e.g. *modern* is an **antonym** of *old-fashioned*.

Apposition

This is a way of adding further information about a noun. The same thing is described in a different way and, in basic **apposition**, this information is simply put after the first noun inside commas:
Global warming is a process that is disputed by many and is …
Global warming, <u>a process that is disputed by many</u>, is …

Auxiliary verb / main or lexical verb

A verb can be one word or several:
She <u>phoned</u> him. (1 word)
I <u>have been phoned</u> by a nuisance caller. (3 words)

When there are several words you can look for a **lexical verb** (sometimes called a **main verb**) and one or more **auxiliary verbs**. The lexical verb gives the meaning and comes at the end. In the first example above there is one lexical verb (*phoned*). In the second example above there are two auxiliary verbs (*have been*) and a lexical verb (*phoned*).

An auxiliary verb comes in front of another verb to give different meanings (e.g. change the tense, or create a question). *Be*, *have* and *do* are the three main verbs used as auxiliaries:
He <u>is</u> leaving.
<u>Do</u> you drink coffee?
He <u>has</u> left.

Modal verbs are also classified as auxiliary verbs.

Clause / sentence

These terms are often used interchangeably and there is a lot of debate about them in grammatical theory. But in a book about writing it is useful to think of a **sentence** as made up of **clauses**. Each clause has one lexical verb and is usually separated from the next by a comma (,) and a co-ordinating word, e.g. *and*:
Thieves stole a painting and some antiques. (1 clause, 1 sentence)
Thieves stole a painting, and drove away at high speed. (2 clauses, 1 sentence)

Many adjectives have **comparative** and **superlative** forms. These exist because the two or more things can be compared in terms of the adjective:

She's <u>tall</u> for her age.
She's <u>taller</u> than her brother. (comparative form)
She's <u>the tallest</u> pupil in class. (superlative form. You need *the* because there's only one tallest pupil!)

Short adjectives are formed with *–er/–est*, as above; longer adjectives use *more* and *the most*:
It's an exciting film.
It's <u>more</u> exciting than the one we saw last week.
It's <u>the most</u> exciting film I've ever seen.

There are a number of irregular forms.

A **complement** is a noun or other phrase needed after a verb to complete the clause. The objects that are needed after a transitive verb are typical examples of complements, but there are a range of other types of verb which force other words to be added:

He lit <u>a match</u>. (transitive verb + noun)
The car was <u>beautiful</u>. (verb *be* used as a lexical verb + adjective)
The crowd became <u>angry</u>. (verb similar to + adjective)

If you stop at the verb, and find you have to ask, for example: 'lit what?', 'was what?, 'became what?' then you are using a verb that takes a complement.

Some verbs also strongly suggest a complement is needed, or have a different meaning without one. These complements are very often prepositional phrases:
I fell. ✓
I fell <u>into a deep sleep</u>. ✓

It is useful to think of nouns as words for things you can count or make plural, and words for ~~things~~ that you can't count:
apple → *apples* (**countable**)
justice → *justices* ✗ (**uncountable**)

However, many uncountable nouns can be used countably, and also the other way round.
The atmosphere<u>s</u> of the planets in our solar system are very different. ('uncountable' noun used countably)
<u>Cloud</u> can reduce visibility very quickly when you are high in the mountains. ('countable' noun being used uncountably)

English nouns are used with articles: *a/the*. The **indefinite** article *a/an* is used with a noun when it does not matter which one you are talking about, or you do not know which one you are talking about:
<u>A</u> thief stole my car.

The **definite** article is used when there is only one of something, or when you know which one of a class of things you are talking about:
<u>The</u> thief who stole my car was caught the next day.

Zero article is used with plural nouns to make a general statement and with nouns that refer to things you can't count or divide up into parts:
(no article) *Diamonds are very expensive.* (= all diamonds)
(no article) *Carbon is the basis of all life on earth.* (= the substance)

Degree adjective

Adjectives give information about the features of a noun. Some features can apply more or less, others are absolute. The first kind are **degree adjectives** and you can test for them by putting *very* in front of the adjective:
He's rich. (You can put *very* in front of *rich* so it's a degree adjective.)
The house is perfect. (You cannot put *very* in front of *perfect*. *Perfect* is an absolute quality.)

Ellipsis

This is a process that happens in both formal and informal writing. Part of a clause which could be there is left out:
He bought a car and (he bought) a house. (You can leave out the second *he bought* because it is understood.)

Finite / non-finite verb or clause

Verbs can be used in **finite** or **non-finite** forms. Finite verbs change to show tense. Non-finite verbs never change, whatever the tense of the main verb in the sentence. There are two forms: *–ing* and the infinitive or base form of the verb:
To see if she was in, he called her on her mobile phone. (base/infinitive form)
Leaving the house at 7.00, I got to the station by 7.30. (–ing form)

Non-finite verbs form the basis of a **non-finite clause**.

Main verb / main v subordinate clause

The term **main verb** is used in two ways. When you are analysing the verb part of a clause, you can distinguish between auxiliary verbs and lexical/main verbs (see separate entry for *auxiliary verb*).

The term main verb is also often used in analysing writing. It means the verb in the sentence that can stand alone, rather than the verb in a dependent (subordinate) clause:
Driving to work one morning (subordinate clause), *I **saw** an accident* (main clause).
*His accent **is** very good* (main clause), *because he lived in France for many years* (subordinate clause).

The clauses that are underlined cannot stand alone and this tells us that the verbs in bold are the main verbs. In formal writing, it is useful to say that a sentence is not complete without a main verb.

Modal / semi-modal verb

A **modal** verb is a special kind of auxiliary verb. Modal verbs – *can, could, will, would, may, might, must* – add meaning to the lexical verb and help it to express ideas of probability, obligation, necessity and so on. Modal verbs do not change to show tense.

Semi-modal verbs give similar meanings, but change to show tense:
We all have to pay taxes.
I had to pay a huge tax bill last year.
I'll have to spend all weekend filling in my tax forms.

Semi-modals can be used in non-finite clauses and as gerunds:
Having to pay taxes is a social obligation
Needing to make a phone call, I stopped my car.

Semi-modals can also be used after standard modals:
You will (modal) have to (semi-modal) see a Doctor.
You might (modal) need to (semi-modal) cancel the agreement.

Semi-modals are also used when a negative form is necessary, but the meaning would change if a modal form was used.
You must not give your username and password to another user.
≠ *You do not have to give your username.*

Passive / active

The focus at the start of a sentence can be on doing an action or receiving an action. This is the distinction between **active** (doing) and **passive** (receiving) in grammatical terms. In the second case you need to create a sentence with a passive verb form. Passive verb forms use the verb *be* and the past participle of the verb:
His car was stolen (passive), *so he rang the police* (active).

Pre-modification

Nouns can be further specified by words that come in front of them. These are generally adjectives or other nouns:
a garden → a big garden (adjective **pre-modification**)
a bridge → a foot bridge (noun pre-modification)

Several words can work together to pre-modify a noun:
A fantastic summer holiday weekend.

Prepositional phrase

Prepositions come before nouns and create **phrases** that function as one grammatical unit.

There are two main uses.

They can add information after a main noun:
The head of the organisation was a woman in her thirties.

They can also give adverbial information, saying where, when, and how an action was carried out:
He dived into the swimming pool, and swam across it with a lot of noise and splashing.

Relative clause / relative pronoun

A **relative clause** adds information after a noun when you want to include a verb. It is linked to a noun by a **relative pronoun** (*which, that, who, whom*):
The couple who bought my house sold it again a month later.

Traditionally, these clauses are divided into defining and non-defining versions. The above is an example of a defining clause. There is no comma between the main noun and the relative pronoun. The clause specifies the couple. You could use the example above in answer to the question 'Which couple?' 'The couple who bought my house'.

Compare this with the following:
The inland revenue, which has recently moved its headquarters to Nottingham, employs several thousand workers.'

Here the relative clause gives non-essential, background information and could easily be left out. It is separated from the noun it refers to by a comma.

A reduced relative clause can be created when the noun is the object of the verb in the clause:

The house which was bought by the American couple is for sale again.

➤ *The house <u>bought by the American couple</u> is for sale again.*

Subject / object

Verbs in English link two parts of the clause together. Usually, these are nouns:

<u>The goalkeeper</u> broke <u>his wrist</u>.

The noun in front of the verb is called the **subject**, and gives the answer to 'Who or what did the action?':

Who broke his wrist? The goalkeeper.

The noun after the verb is called the **object**, and gives the answer to the question 'What did the verb do something to?'

What did he break? He broke his wrist.

Synonym

Word with similar or same meaning, e.g. *big, large.*

Transitive / intransitive verb

Verbs can be categorised according to whether they need an object after them to complete the meaning of the clause or not. Transitive verbs seem unfinished without their object:

He <u>kicked</u> … She <u>threw</u>… (You want to know what was kicked or thrown.)

Intransitive verbs do not seem as unfinished:

The bomb <u>exploded</u>.

In many cases, it is the use in context that defines whether the object is necessary:

He <u>kicked</u> the ball angrily. (transitive use)

He <u>kicked</u> and shouted, and ran away. (Here *kick* is being used intransitively as a self-contained action.)

Index